WITHDRAWAL

BRINGING AMERICA HOME

BRINGING AMERICA HOME

HOW AMERICA LOST HER WAY AND
HOW WE CAN FIND OUR WAY BACK

by *Tom Pauken*

Chronicles Press
Rockford, Illinois
2010

Library of Congress Cataloging-in-Publication Data

ISBN 978-0-9843702-0-7

Bringing America Home is dedicated to our children and grandchildren
in the hope they will rise to the challenge of restoring those
founding principles which made America such a special place.

Let them not be discouraged by the difficult task that awaits them,
but emboldened by the understanding that previous generations of Americans
have successfully met and overcome the great challenges of their times.

May God be with them.

Also by Tom Pauken

The Thirty Years War: The Politics of the Sixties Generation

CONTENTS

HOW AMERICA LOST HER WAY   11

Starting Over   13
The Hijacking of the Conservative Movement   21
Big Government Conservatism Is an Oxymoron   45
The Neoconservative Conquest of American Foreign Policy   57
The Bubble Economy and the Destruction   79
    of the Middle Class
The Coarsening of the Culture   101

FINDING OUR WAY BACK   125

An Overview   127
A New Strategy to Address the Threat of Militant Islam   133
Putting America Back to Work   151
Reforming Our Educational System   169
A Return to Constitutional Principles   179
Traditional Values for a New American Century   197

ABOUT THE AUTHOR   207

BRINGING AMERICA HOME

HOW AMERICA LOST HER WAY

Starting Over

"If stupidity got us into this mess,
then why can't it get us out?"
~Will Rogers

I became actively involved in the conservative movement in 1961 as a 17-year-old college freshman at Georgetown University. Back then, both major political parties accepted the basic premises of modern American liberalism. Liberals believed in a strong executive branch, in an activist federal government that would oversee and direct the American economy, and in a foreign policy of "peaceful coexistence" with the Soviet Union. They also believed in a foreign policy guided by the Wilsonian vision of "making the world safe for democracy." This utopian scheme would be accomplished under the auspices of the United Nations, the successor to the League of Nations. Woodrow Wilson's objective was to establish a lasting peace, but his quest for a New World Order that would end all wars was an abysmal failure.

As I was getting interested in politics, I stumbled across books by conservatives that helped persuade me that liberalism was a flawed political philosophy and presented an alternative view of the proper role of government in our lives that made sense to me and many other young Americans. Among those early readings were *The Conscience of a Conservative* by Barry Goldwater; *Up From Liberalism* by William F. Buckley, Jr.; *The Road to Serfdom* by F.A. Hayek; and *Suicide of the West* by James Burnham. I also had the good fortune to study American government and American political theory at Georgetown University under Dr. George Carey, who, along with the late Willmoore Kendall, gave me an appreciation of the founding principles of the American Republic.

To me, the conservative philosophy had the right answers to the problems our nation faced at that time in our history, and I have been active in the conservative movement ever since.

Looking back, I believed that I was joining the losing side in the battle for America's future when I signed up as a conservative foot soldier. Liberalism had become the dominant ideology on our college campuses and in fashionable intellectual circles. Who would have thought back then that—as Sen. Barry Goldwater was urging—we could put a foreign-policy strategy in place to defeat the Soviet Empire? The attraction of conservatism to so many young people in the early 1960's lay purely in its principles.

Being a conservative certainly was not in vogue with the pre-dominantly liberal mind-set that prevailed at most major universi-ties. At Georgetown University, the Jesuits residing on campus had voted twenty to zero for John F. Kennedy over Richard Nixon in the 1960 presidential election, and conservative Catholic Bill Buckley was not allowed to speak on campus that same year because his views were considered too "radical."

By the time the 1960's rolled around, liberalism had been the dominant ideology among the American intellectual class for decades. Conservatives were not even a majority within the Republican Party. In the early 1960's, the Rockefeller Republicans (representatives of the Wall Street financiers, Big Business, and the Northeastern "elite") were still the most powerful faction in the GOP—and they intended to maintain their grip.

The Rockefeller Republicans (named after their leader, Gov. Nelson Rockefeller of New York) were only slightly less liberal than the liberal Democrats. We Goldwater conservatives called them "liberal lite." The essence of the argument they made for electing liberal Republicans to national office was that they could run the big-government liberal programs more efficiently (and at a lower cost) than the liberal Democrats could.

The Republican establishment seemed to resent Goldwater's very existence. They made fun of his supporters, including some whom they referred to as "little old ladies in tennis shoes." They would learn the hard way in 1964 that they were facing a con-servative grassroots army that the Rockefeller Republicans could not match. Goldwater's book had already prompted a move to nominate him in 1960, but Vice President Richard Nixon had that convention sewn up—and Goldwater knew it. "Grow up, conservatives," Senator Goldwater told the assembled delegates at Chicago's Stockyards. And grow up they did.

While the Rockefeller Republicans took their superiority for granted, thousands of devoted conservatives knocked on doors, licked envelopes, and made phone calls for Barry Goldwater. For the first time in a generation, as Phyllis Schlafly put it, conservatives had "A Choice, Not an Echo." The age of stand-pat "me, too" liberalism ended once Sen. Barry Goldwater defeated Gov. Nelson Rockefeller to win the Republican presidential nomination in 1964. But the assassination of President John F. Kennedy in 1963 derailed Senator Goldwater's challenge to Lyndon Baines Johnson in 1964, and we conservatives found ourselves on the defensive once again after the Johnson landslide in the general election.

Nonetheless, after the disappointing presidencies of Johnson, Richard Nixon, and Gerald Ford, Americans were fed up with liberals. Jimmy Carter won in 1976 only because he was perceived as more conservative than Ford. And 20 years after *The Conscience of a Conservative* first appeared, hard-working conservatives delivered the Republican presidential nomination to Ronald Reagan. Reagan went on to beat President Carter in the general election.

American conservatism had triumphed—or so we thought. In retrospect, though, we can see that conservatism peaked during President Reagan's first term. It enjoyed a brief resurgence in the mid-1990's as the Republicans captured both branches of Congress, but that was just a wave (some call it a tsunami) of anti-Clinton, anti-liberal sentiment in the 1994 election. It did not last. For all practical purposes, the post-Reagan era has been a disappointing period for American conservatives, who had once seemed to be on the verge of restoring and revitalizing a nation that had lost its way in the 1960's and 70's.

In one sense, success has led to our downfall. When conservatives made the Republican Party the majority party in America, the opportunists, pragmatists, and phony conservatives moved in and took control of the Republican Party, and of the conservative movement itself—all in the name of "conservatism."

But what passes for conservatism in the post-Reagan era of

Republican politics is barely recognizable to many of us who were grassroots activists in the early days of the conservative movement—especially after eight years of a Republican administration headed up by George W. Bush, who claimed to be a conservative.

The results were not pretty.

On the domestic scene, the Bush administration failed to act in time to stem the credit and spending excesses of our "bubble economy." While those excesses stem from bad decisions made during the Clinton years by Federal Reserve Chairman Alan Greenspan and Clinton Treasury Secretary Robert Rubin, the Bush administration did nothing to reverse those flawed policies. Now we are paying a heavy economic price for postponing action to deal with what turned out to be a slow-moving train wreck.

The Clinton and Bush administrations also made strategic mistakes in dealing with the threat of militant Islam. And our incoherent and thoughtless policies in Latin America over the past two decades have led to the rise to power of a whole new batch of would-be Fidel Castros. As if that is not bad enough, we have even witnessed the return to power of the discredited Sandinista forces, led by that rather smarmy figure of the left, Daniel Ortega. The Bush administration squandered the political capital built up over three decades of hard work by the Goldwater-Reagan movement. In the process, great damage has been done to the conservative movement, the Republican Party, and our country. That capital is depleted, and we conservatives have to start all over in putting together a set of principled policies to address the enormous economic, foreign-policy, and cultural challenges our nation faces.

The time has come to make it clear that George W. Bush, Karl Rove, Dick Cheney, Paul Wolfowitz, Henry Paulson, and all of the rest do not represent the principles of American conservatism. We should not support Republican candidates for president just because they happen to be the lesser of two evils. That has not worked out well for conservatives in the post-Reagan era of Republican politics.

Nor should we remain silent when a bunch of phony conservatives calling themselves "neoconservatives" hijack the major intellectual organs of the conservative movement and use them to promote their ideological agenda. These former liberal Democrats turned Republicans remind me of Robert McNamara's civilian whiz kids who planned and oversaw our flawed strategy during the Vietnam War. Those intellectuals thought they were a lot smarter and knew a lot more about how to fight the war than our soldiers in Vietnam did. Indeed, the McNamara whiz kids had high IQs, but they were brilliantly wrong. I saw that firsthand as a young military intelligence officer serving in Vietnam. Similarly, the neoconservative architects of George W. Bush's strategy to defeat militant Islam were a group of arrogant intellectuals with very little, if any, military experience. They made things worse, not better, for the soldiers who had to carry out their plans.

Yet even though the foreign-policy predictions of the neoconservative ideologues have been proved wrong time and time again, they continue to impose a foreign-policy litmus test on conservatives. Why do we bother listening to them anymore?

No longer an idealistic 17-year-old college freshman, I am now in my 60's. But I am just as determined today as I was back then, this time to do all that I can to help rebuild what is now only a remnant of a once-powerful conservative movement. Our first goal must be to recapture a Republican Party that has been taken over by Machiavellian pragmatists and neoconservative ideologues, masquerading as "Reagan conservatives." If we can accomplish that formidable task, then we have to provide the American people with the right kind of leadership to get our nation back on the right track. That will not happen with slick political slogans or 30-second sound bites but with a serious assessment of how our leaders have failed us and what is required to make things right. And that assessment can be made only on the basis of principle.

That is what I attempt to do in this book—to make the case for how true conservative principles provide a road map for solving the serious domestic and foreign-policy problems facing our nation, and how those principles can get America back on the right track.

My friend and mentor in business, the late Bill Bowen, liked to use the term "sunk costs" to describe a troubled business investment. As he would point out to me, you cannot undo what already has transpired once you have made a bad investment. You simply have to make the best of a difficult situation. As a businessman, you can either walk away from your investment and accept your business losses, or you can put up additional capital and make necessary changes in an attempt to turn a losing investment into an economic success. It is not easy to try to figure out which is the best course of action in dealing with troubled investments.

Unlike a businessman who has made a bad investment, Americans cannot walk away from the "sunk costs" of failed political leadership. We have to live with the mistakes our political leaders have made and nurse the sick aspects of our ailing country back to health. As Edmund Burke said, we need to treat our ailing country with the love we would show an ailing father. The problems faced by a troubled business are small compared with those that a future conservative president of the United States will confront as he tries to undo the damage done to our country in the post-Reagan period of American politics. The conservative movement has been gravely wounded by wrongheaded decisions made during the presidency of George W. Bush. The economic- and social-conservative majority, which was so much in evidence when I left the Reagan administration at the end of the President's first term, is history. The Democrats now control the White House and hold large majorities in both houses of Congress. Rahm Emanuel, President Obama's White House chief of staff, is intent on ensuring that the current Democratic majority becomes a permanent liberal majority. Meanwhile, our current Republican leaders in Washington, D.C., are floundering, trying to figure out what to do.

Those are our "sunk costs."

We can complain all day long about the failed leadership of our Washington policy makers, Democrats and Republicans alike. And we can bemoan the fact that a liberal Democratic regime, headed by President Barack Obama, has come to power. But that does not help to fix the mess our country is in at the moment.

The problems we face permeate every aspect of our society. The decisions we will make going forward regarding economic and tax policy, the threat of militant Islam, American culture, and our constitutional system will affect all of us—as well as future generations of Americans. The current situation may appear bleak in light of the seriousness of our problems, but it is not hopeless. Nonetheless, we had better get it right. This may be our best—and last—hope to get our nation back on the right track.

Many Americans sense the seriousness of the moment, but they cannot see any solutions on the horizon, which makes it even more serious. What is needed is a new core of grassroots leaders with the dedication and the vision to respond to the crisis facing us.

Americans of goodwill need to join together for the good of the country. This battle for America's future is not a strictly partisan fight. Republican leaders in recent years, particularly during the George W. Bush presidency, have been just as guilty as Democrats like Bill Clinton of focusing on their own short-term political interests rather than on the long-term interests of our country.

We cannot take back the policy mistakes our political leaders have made over the past two decades. But we can begin anew by understanding how America lost her way and how we can find our way back.

Any real progress in making America great again requires addressing the problems of our twin deficits—our huge budget deficits and our trade deficits. It calls for the reassertion of classic traits of the American character—a character that has unfortunately been brushed aside into the shadows since the early 1960's. It calls for policies to rebuild our middle class, the traditional backbone of American society. It requires slowing the growth of government spending and taxation while providing incentives to encourage savings and investment in American businesses and creating jobs here at home. It means addressing responsibly the unfunded liabilities of our entitlement programs. It means recapturing the spirit of sacrifice and the postponement of gratification that are the basis of any free enterprise—and central to the survival of a vibrant society. It means reviving our manufacturing base and the good jobs that sector brings with it. It requires policies that will return us to the "constitutional morality" of our Founding Fathers with their emphasis on checks and balances, separation of powers, and support for the principle of federalism. And it urgently requires the restoration of a culture guided by the principles of Christianity rather than one shaped by what Pope Benedict XVI has called "the dictatorship of relativism."

The Hijacking of the Conservative Movement

*"Every great movement begins as a cause,
becomes a business, and ends as a racket."*
~Eric Hoffer

The modern American conservative movement came of age in the late 1950's and early 1960's. Conservatism at that time stood for the principles of limited government, opposition to international communism, and support for traditional values. The leading political figure of the movement was Sen. Barry Goldwater of Arizona. He warned of the growing centralization of power in America, with special emphasis on the threats posed by the increasing influence of what Goldwater referred to as Big Government, Big Labor, and Big Business. Goldwater was a rugged individualist who believed that the Republican Party should represent what he called the "forgotten Americans"—the middle-class taxpayers and "Main Street" America. While Barry Goldwater lost his race for the presidency against Lyndon Johnson in 1964, he paved the way for Ronald Reagan to lead conservatives to victory in 1980. President Reagan was a principled leader who helped change the world for the better with his successful Cold War strategy to defeat the Soviet Empire and reduce the worldwide influence of international communism. Domestically, Reagan's across-the-board tax cuts in 1981 for individuals and businesses fueled economic growth and job creation that lasted throughout the 1980's and into the early 1990's. While he isn't given enough credit for it, President Reagan also reined in domestic spending during his first term in office while reforming our bloated welfare system.

Unfortunately, conservatives set in motion the seeds of our own destruction during the high point of American conservatism in the 20th century—President Reagan's first term in office. Personnel decisions made at that time have come back to haunt our conservative movement and marginalize conservative influence over policy making in the post-Reagan era of American politics.

The groundwork for the death of the conservative movement was laid by the selection of George Herbert Walker Bush to be Ronald Reagan's vice-presidential running mate in 1980. Upon Reagan's election as president, the mistake was compounded by the choice of Bush's former campaign manager, James Baker, to be the White House chief of staff. Overnight, two of the key leaders of the pragmatic (or "corporate liberal") wing of the Republican Party were in key positions in the administration of a truly conservative president. Moreover, the White House personnel office was headed up by nonconservative Nixon/Ford retreads. This made it more difficult for Reagan conservatives to get hired in an administration headed by a conservative president.

The next major mistake made by the Reagan administration, which would also have long-term consequences for the conservative movement, was the appointment of many neoconservatives to fill key political positions, particularly in foreign policy. For the most part, these were former "social democrats" from the Hubert Humphrey/Scoop Jackson wing of the Democratic Party who had clashed with the anti-Vietnam, left-wing McGovernites during the Cold War period.

As a longtime conservative and as a Reagan official, I not only failed to see the problems these decisions would lead to but was supportive at the time of the selection of Bush as vice president and our outreach to the neoconservatives. It took me a few years to figure out that these were serious mistakes. Personnel is policy, and we would have been better off without the influx of corporate liberals and neocons into positions of influence in the Reagan administration.

There is no doubt about it: The process of changing the face of American conservatism began with Ronald Reagan's fateful decision to select George Herbert Walker Bush as his vice-presidential running mate in 1980. Had Reagan selected someone else, George H.W. Bush never would have been elected president of the United States in 1988. His son, George W. Bush, would not have won election as governor of Texas in 1994 or been elected president of the United States in 2000. Clearly, this fateful decision changed the course of history, as well as the future of American conservatism.

It was a surprise that George H.W. Bush wound up on the ticket with Ronald Reagan in the first place. Bush was not Reagan's first choice, and the Bush selection was strongly opposed by Reagan's supporters in Bush's home state of Texas who had long battled the "Bush wing" of the Texas Republican Party. Their opposition to the "pragmatist wing" of the Republican Party had started with the Goldwater *versus* Rockefeller battle in 1964, and continued with the Reagan *versus* Nixon fight in 1968, the Reagan *versus* Ford campaign in 1976, and the Reagan *versus* Bush race in the 1980 primaries.

Because of pressure building at the Republican National Convention for Reagan to name former president Gerald Ford as his running mate and to bring back Henry Kissinger (the Nixon-Ford foreign-policy chief) to run foreign policy again (something Reagan did not want to see happen), Reagan (at the behest of some of his advisors, including Richard Allen and Ed Meese) opted to go with the "safer choice" of George Bush.

The rest is history.

With George H.W. Bush as vice president and James Baker as White House chief of staff, from day one the Reagan administration was divided into two competing factions—the Reagan conservatives and the Bush/Baker pragmatists. The creative tension between the two competing camps worked reasonably well in the first Reagan term, but it broke down in the final four years of the Reagan presidency as conservatives lost influence to the Bush wing of the Republican Party. In the first term, Reagan conservatives and loyalists held their own in keeping the administration true to the President's conservative roots. Men like William Clark, who served first as deputy secretary of state and later as director of the National Security Council; Bill Casey at the CIA; Cap Weinberger at defense; Ed Meese and Lyn Nofziger at the White House; the supply-side tax cutters at treasury; and solid conservative appointees at various agencies and departments were strongly committed to the implementation of President Reagan's conservative agenda. The Reagan administration remained on course from 1981 through 1984, keeping domestic spending in check, putting in place a strategy to win the Cold War, and passing legislation designed to reduce the heavy burden of taxation on Americans.

23

By the time of Reagan's second term in office, however, a number of factors combined to result in the centrist, pragmatic wing of the Republican Party replacing the Reagan conservatives as the most influential force in the administration.

That shift in power accelerated during George H.W. Bush's only term as president, from 1989 to 1993. The irony is that the American people elected Bush president in 1988 in large part because they believed that he would continue Ronald Reagan's policies. Voting for a Bush presidency was like electing President Reagan to a third term in office—or so most Americans thought. But that was not to be the case. Republican pragmatists and Bush loyalists who had not already managed to get on the federal payroll during the Reagan years flocked to Washington, D.C., to serve in the Bush I administration. Reagan conservatives were systematically rooted out, even if they had supported Bush's candidacy for president in 1988. What mattered more was whether they had been Bush supporters back during the contest for the Republican nomination in 1980. The "Bushies" were far less forgiving than the Reaganites had been when it came to appointing people who were not originally backers of their man. It was as though loyalty to the Bush family was demanded in the same way that loyalty to a royal family might be.

This comment is not meant to cast aspersions on George H.W. Bush, who, in all my personal dealings with him over the years dating back to when I first met him in 1965, has always shown himself to be a true gentleman. There is just something about the Bushes which demands personal loyalty; loyalty to the Bush family and its goals comes first. If loyalty to conservative principles gets in the way, then one is expected to toss those principles overboard and go along with the Bush agenda in order to stay in the good graces of the Bush team.

The problem with George H.W. Bush's brand of pragmatism was well described to me by an old friend of his who had known Bush for a long time. "George sees the greys on virtually every issue. So much so that sometimes he can't distinguish between black and white." That's an apt description of the man. Or, as someone else once said of him, "He has friends who are conservative; he has friends who are liberals. George Bush is with his friends." (I am told that former Senate majority leader Howard Baker used to say the same thing—in jest—about himself.)

There was a certain indecisiveness in President George H.W. Bush's decisionmaking on policy issues which I believe was attributable in part to the fact that Bush was not as philosophically grounded as Reagan was. George Bush and Ronald Reagan wanted to be president for very different reasons. Reagan was a "conviction" politician who ran for president to do something— and he changed the world for the better as a result. My own sense is that George H.W. Bush ran for that office simply to be someone who had achieved the highest office in our land.

When you run for office "to be somebody," it is far easier to justify compromising one's professed political principles ("Read my lips: No new taxes") in order to advance your political career and to win reelection to office. It becomes more about doing what it takes to get elected, rather than standing for principle whatever the consequences.

While President Reagan compromised with the Democratic-controlled Congress, he generally (although not always) reached agreements with the opposition that helped him advance conservative principles. That was not the case with President George H.W. Bush. In instance after instance, President Bush compromised conservative principles in order to get along with the Democratic leaders of Congress. The cynical political reason for compromising was to show the American people that, unlike his right-wing predecessor Ronald Reagan, President Bush was a "compassionate conservative" who could work well with liberals in Congress in a bipartisan fashion. By distancing himself from conservatives, Bush hoped to attract moderate and independent support in his bid for reelection in 1992.

I am sure the Bush political team assumed that conservatives would support Bush's reelection since President Bush was bound to be more conservative (relatively speaking) than any prospective Democratic nominee. Thus, the Republican administration could make its deals with the Democratic-controlled Congress, get the conservatives to hold their noses and vote for Bush in the November election, while picking up political support from moderates and liberals who appreciated Bush's movement away from the conservatives on a number of issues. Not only did that strategy fail to pick up independent voters in the 1992 campaign, President Bush lost the support of much of Reagan's conservative base in that election. Conservatives either stayed home and did not vote, or they expressed their dissatisfaction with Bush's policies by supporting Ross Perot, who received almost 19 percent of the vote in 1992.

During George H.W. Bush's only term as president, the big-business, "corporate liberal" crowd regained its dominance over the decision-making process of the Republican Party. That dominance continued throughout George W. Bush's eight years in the White House.

Yet the neoconservatives wielded very little influence over American foreign policy during the George H.W. Bush administration. President Bush's chief foreign-policy advisor at the National Security Council (NSC) was Gen. Brent Scowcroft, a Kissinger protégé, and James Baker served as secretary of state. Neither Baker nor Scowcroft had much use for the neoconservatives. Like their boss, the key Bush advisors tended to favor a pro-business establishment agenda while also promoting "global capitalism." President Bush's foreign-policy objectives could be summed up in his quest to build a New World Order.

Nonetheless, the George H.W. Bush administration was not reluctant to use military force abroad. The President launched the Persian Gulf War to drive Saddam Hussein out of Kuwait. He approved a military invasion of Panama in 1989 to overthrow Panamanian dictator Manuel Noriega, and he authorized military intervention in Somalia in a so-called humanitarian operation that later went awry.

While the Bush administration intervened militarily to drive Iraqi forces out of Kuwait, it did not attempt to occupy Iraq after defeating Saddam Hussein's military forces. That would have required the stationing of American troops in the Middle East for an interminable period of time, and the administration was reluctant to take that significant step. The President and his chief foreign-policy advisors favored a balanced policy in the Middle East, seeking to preserve Israel's independence while maintaining good relations with our Arab allies in that part of the world.

Neoconservatives were at odds with the administration's foreign policy in the Middle East, but there was little they could do about it. Still, neoconservative leaders took advantage of the post-Reagan period to extend their influence over conservative opinion outlets. They placed their supporters in key positions in academia, the media, and the foundation world, and they increasingly positioned themselves (and those on the right who shared their worldview) to be the "voice of conservatism" to the outside world.

While expanding their control over the conservative intellectual movement, the neoconservatives muffled the voices of their traditionalist and libertarian critics on the right. An agnostic Canadian by the name of David Frum, who briefly served as a speechwriter for President George W. Bush, emerged as the leading "political hitman" for the neoconservatives. Over the years, Frum has savaged the reputations of such conservatives as Pat Buchanan, Robert Novak, Joseph Sobran, Thomas Fleming, Ron Paul, and many others who were not considered sufficiently supportive of the neocon agenda. Frum did much of his dirty work in the pages of such ostensibly conservative publications as *The American Spectator* and *National Review*. Norman Podhoretz, longtime editor of *Commentary* and author of an autobiography entitled *Making It*, was also very active in purging those conservatives who were critics of the neoconservative political agenda from positions of influence in the conservative intellectual movement.

After a while, the center of the conservative movement (which had been so crucial to the intellectual development of the Goldwater-Reagan brand of conservatism) shifted leftward into the hands of erstwhile liberal Democrats whose philosophy was closer to the political liberalism of Woodrow Wilson and Franklin Delano Roosevelt than to the basic conservative beliefs articulated by Barry Goldwater in *Conscience of a Conservative* and Bill Buckley in *Up From Liberalism*.

One of the leading spokesmen for conservatives these days is Charles Krauthammer, a widely syndicated newspaper columnist and a prominent commentator on FOX News. Krauthammer is a former speechwriter for liberal Sen. Walter Mondale, who ran as the Democratic candidate for president against Ronald Reagan in 1984.

The values espoused by Krauthammer and other like-minded neoconservative spokesmen do not reflect traditional conservative principles. Their utopian ideology has more in common with big-government liberalism. Even the slogans associated with their ideology demonstrate this: "democratic globalism," "global democracy," the "global democratic revolution," "the end of history," "American Empire," "national greatness conservatism," "big government conservatism," "making the world safe for democracy," the necessity for "preemptive war" in the Middle East, a go-it-alone attitude in foreign affairs in a "unipolar world" run by the United States, and a permanent U.S. military presence in the Middle East to fight "World War IV."

What is neoconservatism?

For a partial answer to that question, let us turn to the words of the Catholic neoconservative Michael Novak, who gave an interview to *Crisis*, a Catholic journal, about the meaning and historical roots of neoconservatism. Novak has been a resident scholar at the American Enterprise Institute (AEI), the leading neoconservative think tank in America, for over 30 years.

Novak is quite candid in describing the ideology of his fellow neoconservatives. "In the first generation," Novak explains, "virtually all neo-conservatives—Daniel Patrick Moynihan, Irving Kristol, Daniel Bell, Norman Podhoretz, Midge Decter, Richard John Neuhaus, George Weigel, and Paul Johnson in England—were not only Democrats; we were on the left wing of the Democratic Party." When the Vietnam War caused them to turn against the antiwar left, he says, "We considered ourselves to be persons of the Left even as we began to criticize the Left." Novak does not call this development a "turning to the right"; instead, as he puts it, they were "turning against the Left, certainly the far Left" without abandoning their traditional liberal roots. Neoconservatives were known in those days as "social democrats."

These social democrats referred to themselves as Hubert Humphrey Democrats or Scoop Jackson Democrats, but they never were in the camp of the conservative Democrats, even before they drifted into the ascending Republican Party in the late 1970's and early 1980's. In fact, as Jacob Heilbrunn points out in a recent book on the neoconservatives entitled *They Knew They Were Right*, the neocons started out as a "group of brilliant young Trotskyists (in the 1940s) that included Irving Kristol, Seymour Martin Lipset, Nathan Glazer and Melvin Lasky." Many of them later began to call themselves "democratic socialists."

"Many of us once thought that socialism was basically a good idea, but socialists had not found a practical way to implement it successfully," Michael Novak explains. "Then we actually started to examine the many different national experiments in socialism—almost 70. None of them worked. So, socialism cannot be a good idea. Now, if you are on the Left and you cease being a socialist, what are you?" Still, Novak says, "neoconservatives try to imagine, and to work toward, a better future." Like socialists, there is a strong strain of utopianism in their thinking—seeking to make the world a heaven on earth.

Since socialism was a failure, in Novak's case "democratic capitalism" became for him the pathway to that "better future." But he acknowledges that the "social democrats" turned "neoconservatives" did not change their basic philosophy. Their differences with liberals are more like a quarrel between two branches of liberalism.

The British philosopher John Gray points out the critical difference between modern conservatism and the utopian impulse of neoconservatism: "For much of the twentieth century, the conservatives acted as a brake on collectivism. The Conservative party existed to oppose not just socialism but also—and more relevantly—any further advance toward social democracy." But Gray notes that, unlike traditional conservatives, neoconservatives "are unwilling to rely on social evolution" or change in an orderly fashion: "In its enthusiasm for revolutionary change, neo-conservatism has more in common with Jacobinism and Leninism than with neo-liberalism or traditional conservatism."

The neoconservative goal of imposing democracy everywhere in the world is the kind of utopian vision generally associated with the left. It is akin to the Marxist objective of creating a "perfect world."

True conservatives are wary of utopianism and skeptical of man-made schemes to transform human nature. Our philosophical roots are very different from those of the neoconservatives. We believe in the doctrine of original sin, the imperfectibility of human nature in this life, a cyclical view of history, separation of governmental powers, and the principle of subsidiarity. Conservatives also have historically held to the view that military force should be used only when it is in our vital national interest to do so and the cause for taking military action is a just one.

Neoconservatives may have had only marginal influence over American foreign policy during the administrations of Ronald Reagan and George H.W. Bush. But that changed with the election of George W. Bush to the presidency in November 2000.

With the younger Bush's election came all the elements of the perfect storm to kill the conservative movement: the rise to power of Machiavellian pragmatists such as Karl Rove along with neoconservative foreign-policy advisors like Paul Wolfowitz and Douglas Feith under the sponsorship of Vice President Dick Cheney. The new Bush administration might as well have hung out a shingle: "No Goldwater/Reagan conservatives need apply."

An unbelievable set of circumstances resulted in George W. Bush becoming president of the United States, a job for which he was ill suited. It began with his successful quest to get elected governor of Texas. Bush would not even have run for governor in 1994 had independent oilman Clayton Williams not lost narrowly to Democrat Ann Richards in the 1990 gubernatorial campaign.

With Karl Rove as his chief political advisor, George W. Bush laid the groundwork for his run against incumbent Ann Richards by moving to Dallas and becoming the public face of the Texas Rangers Major League Baseball team. Bush held the title of managing general partner of the franchise, but he was only a minor investor in the team. The real decision makers were Tom Schieffer, who ran the day-to-day operations of the business, and Rusty Rose, a hard-nosed Dallas investor, who was the major "money" man in the deal. George W. Bush became the chief spokesman for the Rangers—a role which would establish him in the eyes of Texans as a successful businessman and a sports enthusiast. Bush did a terrific job as "Mr. Outside" for the franchise. The engaging side of his personality came to the fore in this role, and his true love of the game of baseball (one which he had nourished ever since playing Little League as a youngster in Midland) was obvious to anyone who paid attention. In due course Bush's name was seriously floated for the position of baseball commissioner, a job Bush probably would have won had he campaigned for it.

George W. Bush might have made a terrific Major League Baseball commissioner, but he was a lousy president of the United States. He made a mess of things in his eight years in the White House—leaving the conservative movement, the Republican Party, and the country at large in a shambles as he left office in January 2009.

How did it come to this?

One of the Bush sons was expected to redeem the Bush family name by winning back the White House, which had been captured in 1992 by Bill Clinton, who defeated the senior Bush. It turned out to be the eldest son, George W. Bush. George H.W. Bush supporters viewed Bill Clinton as little more than an interloper. The staunch Bush backers believed that Clinton defeated Bush only because of the entry into the race of a third-party candidate, Dallas businessman Ross Perot. (Post-election analysis indicated otherwise, but that was the prevalent opinion of Bush Republicans as to why their man had lost.) Conservatives, on the other hand, attributed Bush's defeat to his abandonment of Reagan's conservative principles—the classic example being George H.W. Bush's pledge at the Republican National Convention ("Read my lips: No new taxes"), which he abandoned once in office.

Two of the Bush sons ran for governor of their respective states in 1994. Most political observers expected that Jeb Bush, a "policy wonk" who was elected governor of Florida in 1994, would be the son to follow his father into the White House. Jeb's older brother, George W., was viewed as a more limited candidate for national office and appeared to have the tougher race against a seemingly popular Texas governor, Ann Richards. Moreover, George W. had not defined himself on policy matters as his brother had over the years. Other than having a generally pro-business, pro-energy perspective, George W. Bush did not come across to political activists in Texas as having any deep-seated convictions.

A lot of reporters (and, perhaps, even the Richards campaign itself) made the mistake of concluding that, since he was not all that interested in issues, George W. Bush must not be very bright. That myth of a lack of intelligence carried over into his tenure as president. Those Bush critics obviously had not done their homework or known George W. Bush that well. He did not get into Yale University simply on his family name. He may not have excelled academically at Andover, the preparatory school he attended; but he scored reasonably high on his college entrance exams. George W. Bush scored 1206 on his SAT, higher than John Kerry's score of 1190. Bush's problem in this regard is a different one, as columnist Joe Sobran has observed: "George W. Bush probably was the kind of student at Yale University who partied all the time, went to ball games, and crammed for exams the night before his tests." Having known George since we were both young men, I never thought he suffered from a lack of intelligence, just that he never exhibited much of an interest in political issues, not even the most volatile issue of our generation—the war in Vietnam. I simply did not consider George to be a serious man at the time when I first met him during our college years. Nothing since then has caused me to change my initial impression of him.

Even after college and a stint in the National Guard during the Vietnam War, George W. Bush gave no indication that he had changed and developed even a passing interest in domestic or international issues. Although his "political handlers" (particularly Karl Rove) liked to compare him to conservative favorite Ronald Reagan, the two men were not even remotely similar. Reagan truly was a man of ideas, a conviction politician who had a strategic vision which shaped his worldview. Reagan did much of his own research into issues over the years and wrote most of his speeches before his election as president. He was well read and had a clear understanding of conservative intellectual thought. I can't imagine George W. Bush ever doing his own research or writing any of the speeches he gave in public. He read what others prepared for him. George W. Bush was a front man in his political career just as he had been the front man for the Texas Rangers baseball franchise.

And that was just the way his political mentor, Karl Rove, liked it. Rove would be the power behind the throne, and George W.

would be the public face. Rove and Bush were a good match for each other. Like his mentor, Bush was far more interested in the "game" of politics, getting elected and being politically popular, than in making a difference on the policy front. Although the two men had dramatically different backgrounds, Rove and Bush fed into each other's insecurities. Bush was bothered that he did not seem to measure up to his father. His successful political career was his way to prove that he was just as good a politician as his father was (if not better) and, thus, just as good a man.

Karl Rove was a college dropout who began his political consulting career in Texas thanks to George H.W. Bush. Rove fought his way up through the rough-and-tumble world of the "hired guns" of American politics, and George W. Bush became Karl's ticket to the top. A man with many acquaintances but few friends, Rove was a total "political animal." Rove's political bible is Machiavelli's *Prince*, which preaches the "gospel" of the amorality of politics. While often compared to the late Lee Atwater (who also began his career in politics as a College Republican activist), Rove could not be more different. Lee Atwater was the kind of political consultant who would fight hard for his candidate, but he never held grudges if you happened to be working for a different candidate in that particular Republican primary. After the race was over, Lee would say, in effect, that while we may have had our differences in this race, we will be on the same side in the future, so let's put these differences behind us. Lee Atwater did not burn bridges behind him unnecessarily.

Karl Rove is just the opposite. When Bush was governor, you either supported the Bush-Rove agenda as a Texas Republican, or you were viewed as disloyal and wound up on Karl Rove's enemies list. Rove was a control freak who wanted malleable conservatives whom he could co-opt and who would be indebted to him as George W. Bush became more powerful politically. Having stopped saluting involuntarily when I left the U.S. Army after returning from Vietnam, I was not inclined to simply toe the party line when matters of substantive policy were at stake. I had been elected Republican state chairman of Texas in 1994 in spite of strong, private opposition from Bush and Rove. Even though I helped marshal our grassroots conservatives behind George W. Bush in his campaign for governor, it did not matter to Bush and Rove. I already was on Rove's enemies list and would remain there throughout my three years in office.

Feeding off each other's insecurities, the Bush-Rove combination reminded me of the mind-set that was so prevalent in the Nixon administration, a paranoia that led the people in charge to believe that anyone who was not "with us" had to be an enemy. I knew what that felt like during my time as Texas Republican state chairman when Bush was governor. Fred Barnes, the editor of *The Weekly Standard*, did not have to remind me of the difficult situation I was in when he called to tell me that Bush and Rove had described me as their "least favorite Republican in Texas."

At the same time, I have to give Karl Rove the lion's share of the credit for getting George W. Bush elected as governor of Texas in 1994 and as president of the United States in 2000. Rove had a "will to power." He ran Bush's campaign for governor in 1994, was the first among equals as an advisor to Bush during his tenure as governor of Texas, and ran Bush's presidential campaign against Steve Forbes and John McCain in the primary election and against Al Gore in November. When Bush was running for president, Rove sold Republicans and the mainstream media on the idea that George W. Bush's political views were closer to Ronald Reagan's than to his own father's. That was not the case, but it worked. Many conservatives thought that George W. Bush was one of their own.

While George W. Bush enjoyed the support of most of his father's major financial backers, he also benefited enormously from the power of being governor of Texas and the contributions that naturally flowed to the governor from those with an interest in the affairs of state government. Karl Rove was expert at reaching out to those big-dollar givers and getting them to back his boss in his presidential bid.

Even though neither Rove nor George W. Bush had much support from grassroots conservatives, Rove employed a top-down approach to win conservative support. A religious agnostic, Rove was surprisingly adept at mobilizing evangelical conservatives behind the Bush campaign for president. Karl got Ralph Reed, the former leader of the Christian Coalition, put on Enron's corporate payroll as a "consultant," which freed Reed up to work for Bush's nomination in 2000. Reed helped deliver social conservatives. Rove also worked hard to cultivate the political support of evangelical leaders such as Pat Robertson and Jerry Falwell and succeeded in getting these prominent social conservatives to endorse Bush.

Rove's strategy worked as enough conservatives joined the more centrist Bush Republicans to win the Republican nomination for George W. Bush.

Karl Rove had become the indispensable man; by mid-2002 (with George W. in the White House) he had already become known by Washington insiders as "King Karl" or "Bush's Brain" (the title of the book by Wayne Slater and James Moore). Winning the governorship of Texas in 1994 was the key to all that would follow in George W. Bush's rise to power.

I had been elected Republican state chairman in Texas in 1994 when Bush ran for governor, and you could feel the strong anti-Clinton, anti-Richards mood at the grassroots level during that election cycle. We had a bumper sticker which read: "Stop Clinton, Vote Republican"; and we could not print them fast enough to satisfy the demand. Richards had managed to alienate both the economic and the social conservatives during her first term in office, and conservative activists in Texas were determined to do whatever it took to defeat her. Her strong commitment to feminist issues made her exceedingly unpopular in pro-life, pro-family circles. Second Amendment supporters were angry at Clinton and Richards for pushing gun control.

But Governor Richards' biggest mistake was in pushing a school-finance scheme known as the "Robin Hood" plan, which transferred property taxes from so-called property-rich districts to property-poor districts. This required a constitutional amendment that had to be approved by Texas voters. Initially, it appeared that this would be no problem for Richards; she raised a substantial war chest from the usual corporate suspects (who wanted to stay on the good side of the governor) to sell this plan to Texans. But Texas voters weren't buying. I organized a group called Texans Against Robin Hood Taxes to defeat the amendment; before long, opposition to the Richards plan had sprung up all over the state. By the time of the election in the summer of 1993, people came out in droves to vote the plan down by a margin of two to one. I was on a split-screen TV interview with Governor Richards that evening, and she had a shocked look on her face as she commented on the devastating loss she had suffered as the principal proponent of "Robin Hood." The political career of Ann Richards started to unravel that evening.

I was not the only one to notice. George W. Bush later remarked that, watching her on TV that night, he sensed her vulnerability for the first time. Bush, who had stayed out of the campaign against "Robin Hood," nonetheless used the issue effectively against Ann Richards during his campaign for governor. For even though the constitutional amendment went down to defeat, Richards and her allies in the legislature resurrected "Robin Hood" and passed a legislative version that they claimed did not require voter approval.

In a way, the defeat of Bush's father blazed the path for George W. Bush's victory as governor of Texas in 1994. The Reagan coalition of economic and social conservatives had come unglued during George H.W. Bush's presidency. Bill Clinton came to office in January 1993. With the assistance of his wife Hillary, President Clinton managed to reenergize the economic and social conservatives against the Democrats by promoting socialized medicine, higher taxes, homosexuals in the military, unlimited abortion rights, and gun control. Ann Richards managed to do the same in Texas with her liberal positions on social issues and her school-finance redistribution scheme. By their rhetoric and actions, liberal Democrats like Bill Clinton and Ann Richards put the Reagan coalition of economic and social conservatives back together again—against them.

Rove ran a well-scripted campaign for Bush that was relatively error-free while Richards seemed a lackluster candidate in the 1994 election. The mood of Texas voters worked in Bush's favor, and George W. won a relatively easy victory while his brother Jeb was a surprising loser in the Florida gubernatorial race to Democrat Lawton Chiles. All of a sudden, George W. Bush was positioned to be the next Bush to make a bid for the White House.

It was evident from the very beginning of George W. Bush's first term as governor that his sights were set higher and that his actions as governor were designed to further his presidential ambitions. During the course of his gubernatorial campaign, Bush had gained the unofficial support of the powerful Democratic Lt. Gov. Bob Bullock. Once in office, Bush made it clear that he would work closely with Bullock to forge a bipartisan consensus on the issues. That played well with the Texas public and the Austin-based journalists who covered state government, but it meant in effect that Bullock, a centrist Democrat, would remain in control of policy matters while Bush would get credit for passage of legislation that advanced his campaign agenda of tort reform, welfare reform, education reform, and reform of the criminal-justice system. During the first legislative session with Bush as governor, bills were passed which addressed all of these issues. When it came to policy changes in these areas, however, the real decision maker was Lt. Gov. Bob Bullock, not Gov. George W. Bush. Bullock simply allowed Bush to take credit for the changes, most of which were not all that significant from a conservative perspective. The exception was in the area of tort reform. There, Bush and his backers had a strong personal interest.

The one issue that Bush refused to touch was the "Robin Hood" school-finance legislation which had been backed by both Ann Richards and Bob Bullock. Nonetheless, it looked like Bush would have to tackle this issue anyway. A challenge to the legislation was making its way to the Texas Supreme Court, and a new Republican majority on the court seemed poised to declare "Robin Hood" unconstitutional. It appeared that there were at least five votes (a majority) on the court who thought "Robin Hood" an unconstitutional violation of the prohibition against a statewide property tax. Unfortunately for Texans, John Cornyn reversed himself on this issue from a previous opinion. Instead, by a five-to-four vote, the court voted to uphold the constitutionality of "Robin Hood."

Cornyn's reversal made it possible for Bush and Rove to lay the groundwork for Bush's run for the White House in 2000 without being distracted—and possibly derailed—by this powerful and sensitive issue that, more than any other, had defeated Ann

Richards and put Bush in the governor's mansion.

The election of George W. Bush as president in 2000 gave us the worst of both worlds. Coming back to power were the Machiavellian pragmatists led by Karl Rove, the President's campaign manager and chief political advisor. They were joined by the neoconservative advocates of a military interventionist policy in the Middle East, whose principal sponsor would turn out to be Vice President Dick Cheney. While Rove oversaw politics and much of the decision making with respect to domestic policy, Vice President Cheney became the *de facto* president of foreign policy in the first Bush term.

The ascent of Karl Rove to the pinnacle of power in the Bush administration shows the dangers of putting political consultants in charge of policy. His prominent influence over domestic policy in Bush's first term paved the way for the rise of "big government conservatism" and the abandonment of the conservative principles of limited government and federalism. From Karl's perspective, there was nothing wrong with big government now that he and his cronies were in power.

The Goldwater-Reagan brand of conservatism has fallen on hard times in the post-Reagan era, losing influence to a powerful coalition of neoconservatives and Republican pragmatists. A philosophy which held that power is best reserved to the states, the local communities, and the people themselves has been supplanted by big-government conservatism here at home and a national-greatness conservatism abroad that seeks to use American military force to expand global democracy. This brand of false conservatism maintains that increasing the power and reach of the federal government is fine so long as "our people" are in charge and "our policies" are being pursued. This is a far cry from the principles enunciated by our Founding Fathers in the *Federalist* (the theoretical underpinning of the U.S. Constitution), which articulated the inherent danger of an excessive concentration of economic and political power. Instead, big-government conservatism represents the return of the old "spoils" system of the big spenders, camouflaged as "reform" in the name of "compassionate conservatism."

Stressing the importance of controlling federal spending and warning of the dangers of excessive budget deficits was considered outdated by those running the Bush White House. In response to a question about high budget deficits, Vice President Cheney declared, "Deficits don't matter." Annual budget deficits of $500 billion or more and trade deficits in excess of $800 billion annually were run up during the Bush presidency—and that was in supposedly good economic times. At the time, I asked what would happen when we slid into a recession and government tax revenues declined. We learned the answer to the question in the last year of Bush's second term when the national economic hurricane hit, and the budget deficit came in at $1.2 trillion in Fiscal Year 2009—and that was before Congress passed the Obama stimulus plan, resulting in a $2 trillion budget deficit for FY 2010.

How long can we depend on foreign central banks—particularly those of China and Japan—continuing to buy U.S. dollars to fund our budget and trade deficits? The Bush administration's "guns and butter" spending policy was eerily reminiscent of the excesses of the Lyndon Johnson administration back during the Vietnam War. Stagflation was the result then, and that combination of an inflationary environment with slowing economic growth is back.

While administration economic spokesmen (and their Wall Street allies) herald the virtues of free trade in both the Bush and Obama administrations, our trade deficits have soared to record levels over the past decade. And our manufacturing base is being hollowed out.

Even service-related jobs are being outsourced to workers in foreign lands. Every trading country in the world—except the United States—has a tax system designed to protect its domestic businesses. Yet the United States relies on a corporate income tax that has built-in incentives for American corporations to export jobs overseas. That same corporate tax system rewards American companies that leverage their assets by loading them up with high levels of corporate debt. At the same time, our business tax system penalizes companies with clean balance sheets, and little or no corporate debt, by taxing them at a higher percentage rate.

On a personal level, Americans are losing their traditional aversion to high levels of personal debt. People of my parents' generation, who lived through the Great Depression of the 1930's, experienced firsthand the economic devastation wrought by the credit excesses of the Roaring 20's. People of that generation preached the virtues of thrift and generally followed their own advice by paying off the debt on their home so that they would own it free and clear while saving for their retirement years. What will this generation, much more self-indulgent than that of the 1930's, do when hard times come? We lack the good habits and salutary virtues of that generation. Nor are our roots as strong today as they were back then when there was more of a sense of community, intact families, and a solid work ethic. Without those values to help them get through the economic crisis, that generation would have sunk into chaos. What about ours?

The importance of thrift was ingrained in the mind-set of the World War II generation. That is no longer the case. We save too little, and too many Americans these days are saddled with excessively high levels of credit-card debt along with mortgage obligations on their residences that leave them with little or no equity in their own homes. The so-called ownership society runs the risk of becoming what investor Warren Buffet calls a "sharecropper's society" as current trends play out to their logical conclusion in the "housing bubble." Home prices, which rose 85 percent in the United States from 1997 to 2006, have dropped more than 15 percent since then and undoubtedly have farther to fall.

Since the days when Earl Warren was Chief Justice of the U.S. Supreme Court, sitting federal judges with lifetime tenure have shown an increasing proclivity to substitute their own will for the will of our elected legislative bodies on a wide range of political questions—frustrating a majority of Americans who feel we have no recourse against the decisions of these unelected judges who have such enormous political power. Yet our political leaders in the executive and legislative branches of the federal government do little to curb this abuse of judicial power, even though a legislative solution is available that would solve most of these problems of judicial overreach. What happened to our once-vibrant recognition that our constitutional form of government was critical to our survival as a free society over the past two centuries?

And whatever became of our "constitutional morality?" In the years since the founding, the intimate connection between morality and freedom has been repeatedly underscored.

John Adams said, "We have no constitution that functions in the absence of a moral people." The authors of the *Federalist* emphasized that the success of our democratic republic depended on us remaining a virtuous people. Words attributed to Alexis de Tocqueville, author of *Democracy in America*, reflect that sentiment: "America is great because she is good and if she ever ceases to be good, she will cease to be great."

John Courtney Murray wrote about the political principles of our Founding Fathers in his landmark book *We Hold These Truths*: "For the pragmatist there are, properly speaking, no truths; there are only results. But the American Proposition rests on the more traditional conviction that there are truths; that they can be known; that they must be held; for, if they are not held, assented to, consented to, worked into the texture of institutions, there can be no hope of founding a true City, in which men may dwell in dignity, peace, unity, justice, well-being, freedom."

That is why the Christian ethic is at the core of the belief system of a truly free society.

Issues such as respect for the life of the unborn; the defense of the family, as represented by the marriage between a man and a woman; and the recognition that God should not be excluded from the public square are not peripheral but are key ingredients in the preservation of a free society.

Where are our political leaders using their bully pulpit to speak out against the coarsening of our culture, particularly fueled by Hollywood elites openly hostile to our traditional religious beliefs? The entertainment industry transmits to the world (as well as to us here at home) its interpretation of "American values," which often degenerates into mindless hedonism. Hollywood is dominated by a mind-set aptly described by Pope Benedict XVI as a "dictatorship of relativism."

We need to encourage those filmmakers and talented artists who are trying to make a positive difference with respect to our culture. Commercially successful movies that respect faith, such as *The Passion of the Christ* and *The Chronicles of Narnia*, offer encouraging signs that a new counterculture may yet challenge the Hollywood culture.

The primary threat to Western civilization during the 20th century was international communism; that threat was overcome in large part thanks to the strategy put in place by President Reagan to defeat the Soviet Empire.

Now, the principal strategic threat in our times is militant Islam—which poses an even greater threat to our way of life. It is ludicrous, however, to think that the most effective means of addressing that threat is by imposing democracy on the Middle East through military force, or by persuading Muslims of the benefits of Western-style materialism.

The neoconservative strategy of using U.S. military force to impose democracy on the Middle East is not working. Instead, it is fanning the flames of militant Islam. A continuation of our present strategy will further destabilize the Middle East and turn more Muslims into Al Qaeda supporters. We are playing into the hands of Osama bin Laden and furthering his objectives of radicalizing the Middle East.

The time has come to go back to the drawing board and to rethink our strategy for countering the threat of militant Islam.

When President Reagan assumed the presidency in January 1981, he moved quickly to change the direction of our economic and foreign policy. He believed that ideas have consequences, and he proved that ideas can change the world. The times are not the same as they were then. The problems of our nation are different now; indeed, they are much more serious. Nonetheless, our conservative principles are just as valid today as they were then, and they can provide the underpinning for a coherent strategy to help America find her way back.

The Republican Party needs to become, once again, a party guided by basic conservative principles. We need to think about more than just the next election—or what the polls say we should do. Instead, we need to make decisions based on what is good for our country in the long term. If we provide that kind of leadership, I am confident that the American people will rally behind us.

Big Government Conservatism Is an Oxymoron

"Government always finds a need
for whatever money it gets."
~Ronald Reagan

When Ronald Reagan was elected president of the United States in 1980, he referred to our nation's capital, Washington, D.C., as a swampland and urged his appointees in the federal government to help him "drain the swamps." As my friend and fellow conservative Stan Evans likes to say, the problem was that, after a while, the swamp began to feel more like a hot tub for a number of the President's appointees.

I saw that firsthand as the head of an independent federal agency known then as Action. The agency had been established in the Kennedy/Johnson years as the Office of Economic Opportunity (OEO). OEO became a major funding source for the "poverty pimps," primarily East Coast-based consultants who got large government grants to fight the "War on Poverty." Many of the so-called poverty warriors got rich off taxpayer dollars, but very little of the money trickled down to the poor people the agency was supposed to help. By the late 60's, it had become a hotbed for the newly fashionable radicals of that decade.

Then Richard Nixon came to town and vowed to cut OEO's budget. Howard Phillips, the first director he appointed to head OEO, tried to do just that, but he did not last long. Phillips was replaced by Congressman Don Rumsfeld. Rumsfeld made Dick Cheney his chief of staff and brought along a team of loyalists to take control of the agency. Both Rumsfeld and Cheney understood intuitively the ways of Washington. One does not get ahead by cutting spending and reducing the federal bureaucracy. OEO avoided the chopping block, and the Washington careers of Rumsfeld and Cheney took off.

Ironically, when the George W. Bush administration turned out to be a failure, "conservatism" got the blame even though Rumsfeld and Cheney (like so many others who served in George W. Bush's administration) had been part of the anti-Reagan wing of the Republican Party.

By the time I took over as director in 1981, OEO had changed its name to Action and had a $160 million budget and a thousand employees. It may have been a small swamp by Washington standards, but Reagan was right: It was still a swamp, and a messy one at that. We cut the budget from $160 million to $120 million, the staff from 1,000 to 500, and accomplished a lot more with a lot less money. Our efforts to cut the bureaucracy even more were blocked by Lowell Weicker, the liberal Republican senator from Connecticut who was the subcommittee chairman overseeing Action.

Today, Action is called AmeriCorps and spends far more money than ever after eight years of Republican control of the executive branch under George W. Bush. Its budget in FY 2009 was more than $888 million—nearly eight times higher than when I exited the agency in 1985.

What happened at Action is not an isolated example of a failed attempt to rein in federal spending. A number of Reagan appointees took seriously the President's call to cut wasteful federal spending and reduce the burden of federal regulations. I think particularly of Don Devine at the Office of Personnel Management (OPM), Ray Donovan at the Department of Labor, and James Watt and Don Hodel at the Department of the Interior. Yet each was subjected to negative attacks in the media instigated by those in Washington determined to preserve federal spending. Meanwhile, those who made their peace with the status quo were treated favorably in the mainstream media and furthered their own careers.

Too many of the agency and department heads, even in the Reagan administration, fell in love with their agency or department and became captured by the permanent bureaucracy. They wound up defending their "turf" and the spending needs of their particular department instead of cutting federal spending. Yet, in spite of all of these hurdles, overall domestic spending during the first Reagan term was kept under control, a fact not generally acknowledged by the liberal critics of the Reagan presidency. It was only in Reagan's second term that the Washington establishment begin to regain control of the reins of the federal government. Domestic federal spending has not stopped growing ever since.

Even given the missed opportunities to get federal spending under control, for conservatives the 1980's were the good old days compared to four years of George H.W. Bush, eight years of Bill Clinton, eight years of George W. Bush, and the first year of the Obama administration. Federal spending and unfunded federal mandates on state and local governments are completely out of control. Is there any hope whatsoever that a true federalist could actually get elected president, reduce the growth of federal spending, and return power to the states, local communities, and the people?

The Republican Party of Barry Goldwater and Ronald Reagan was a conservative party of limited government. That all changed in the post-Reagan era of Republican politics. The George W. Bush presidency embraced the philosophy of "big government conservatism." That ideology has more in common with the New Deal of Franklin Delano Roosevelt and the Great Society of Lyndon Baines Johnson than with the conservative philosophy of Barry Goldwater and Ronald Reagan.

Fred Barnes, the editor of the leading neoconservative magazine *The Weekly Standard*, described the Bush philosophy of "big government conservatism" in a article in the *Wall Street Journal* in the summer of 2003. According to Barnes, the Bush administration believed "in using what would normally be seen as liberal means—activist government—for conservative ends. And they're willing to spend more and increase the size of government in the process." In the same article, Barnes noted that "big government conservatives are favorably disposed toward what neoconservative Irving Kristol has called a 'conservative welfare state.'" Then, in an understatement, Barnes added: "Neocons tend to be big government conservatives." Barnes has lauded Bush for embracing this new brand of "conservatism."

A cynic might suggest that what Barnes was really saying was that there is nothing wrong with big government so long as "our guys" are in charge.

As Fred Barnes acknowledged, there was a "surge of federal spending" during Bush's presidency, resulting in "swollen deficits." (A Cato Institute study refers to Bush as "the biggest spending President in 30 years.") President Bush completely failed to exercise his veto power during his first term in office. The President even teamed up with Teddy Kennedy to ensure the passage of his "No Child Left Behind" legislation, which expanded the federal role in education beyond the wildest dreams of diehard liberals. Moreover, President Bush sought, and received from Congress, the first extension of entitlements (in this case, Medicare entitlements) since the Johnson administration in the 1960's.

Yet back in 2003 none of these spending excesses seemed to trouble Barnes or his fellow neoconservatives. They were just as supportive of the President's domestic spending as they were enthusiastic about his decision to go to war with Iraq.

The Economist had a very different take on the President in a cover story around the same time: "Is George Bush a socialist?" The article compared Bush's reckless spending policies to the "guns and butter" spending excesses of Lyndon B. Johnson's administration.

For example, the budget of the Department of Education more than doubled during George W. Bush's tenure. Floyd Norris of the *New York Times* even noted (February 9, 2008) that "George W. Bush had the dubious distinction of being the first president since World War II to preside over an economy in which federal government employment rose more rapidly than employment in the private sector."

At President Bush's insistence, Congress narrowly passed a huge new Medicare entitlement for prescription drugs. The Medicare system already was running unsustainable deficits. According to economists Jogadeesh Gokhale and Kent Smetters, Medicare held $62 trillion in unfunded liabilities as of 2005 — 8.5 times as much as the unfunded liabilities of Social Security. In an article for the *Wall Street Journal* entitled "Medicare Meltdown" (May 8, 2007), public trustee of the Social Security and Medicare system Thomas R. Saving warned that "within seven years Medicare taxes will fall short of Medicare expenses by more than 45%."

48

The situation in 2008 was even worse. According to Congressman Jeb Hensarling, "Medicare trustees say that the unfunded obligations of the system amount to more than $74 trillion—six times greater than the current size of the American economy."

This projected shortfall in Medicare funding grows by two trillion dollars each year. At the current rate, the Medicare Part A trust fund will run out of money by 2019.

The Medicare program is heading for bankruptcy, and the President's chief political advisor Karl Rove sped up the day of reckoning by adding a new entitlement in order to help President Bush win reelection in 2004. Rove pressured Republicans in Congress to go along on the theory that this was the price they had to pay in order to reelect the President.

Sound economic policy was sacrificed on the altar of short-term political gain. This buying of political support with taxpayers' money brings to mind the words of Alexis de Tocqueville in *Democracy in America*: "The American Republic will endure until the day Congress discovers that it can bribe the public with the public's money."

Of course, there was vigorous dissent, led by longtime conservative leader Don Devine, who had been director of the Office of Personnel Management in the Reagan administration. Many conservatives joined Devine, but their efforts were unsuccessful. So, too, were conservative campaigns to block Bush's costly "No Child Left Behind" education bill, which came loaded with unfunded federal mandates. Nor have conservatives such as Jeb Hensarling in the House and Tom Coburn in the Senate been able to curtail earmarks that bloat federal spending. Generally, any serious attempts to slow the growth in federal spending and keep it within reasonable limits have failed miserably in spite of the fact that Republicans controlled both houses of Congress until 2007. Republicans in Congress did a better job of controlling federal spending when Bill Clinton and the Democrats controlled the White House.

When you start adding up the spending excesses of the George W. Bush administration, the numbers are scary. We are approaching a trillion dollars on the war in Iraq, with little to show for it.

With the President's support, Congress passed in 2006 a $286.4 billion transportation bill loaded with pork. Our annual budget deficits ran in excess of $300 billion at a time when our economy was in good shape. With the passage of the Bush economic stimulus package in 2008, the budget deficit was expected to exceed $500 billion in FY 2009.

Then things got much worse as an economic hurricane—fueled by credit excess, cheap money (the result of artificially low interest rates set by Fed Chairmen Alan Greenspan and Ben Bernanke), and excessive government spending—hit our shores in the fall of 2007. The anticipated $500 billion deficit turned into a projected $1.2 trillion one. That does not include the trillions of additional dollars given out to troubled financial institutions by the Bush and Obama administrations. Moreover, that $1.2 trillion deficit was before the Democratic majority in Congress passed another $800 billion stimulus package in 2008, raising the projected federal deficit in FY 2010 to $2 trillion. Where is the money going to come from?

Meanwhile, many of our states suddenly find themselves in a budget shortfall. California is worst off, with a $42.5 billion budget deficit as of January 2009. Only Texas, of all of the large states in the country, began 2009 with a substantial budget surplus. All together, 44 states were running budget deficits, while only 6 states had a surplus as we headed into 2009.

On top of all of these deficits at the federal and state levels of government, local taxing bodies around the country have run out of money to spend; some are effectively bankrupt. And these budget deficit figures don't take into account our trade deficits, which were running $700 to $800 billion annually until the U.S. economy crashed in 2008.

The big-government crowd in Washington and elsewhere are bankrupting our country. And Republicans are just as culpable as Democrats in treating our taxpayer dollars as "other people's money" to be spent as they and the special interests decide. If this is what "conservatism" has come to mean—spending whatever it takes to get and maintain power–then we might as well officially commemorate the death of conservatism. Americans at the grassroots level had better wake up and realize that they have been bamboozled by the Washington establishment, which maintains control of the reins of government no matter which party is in control of the White House.

Fortunately, in my own state of Texas, Republican Gov. Rick Perry and the Republican-controlled Texas legislature have kept the growth of state spending at reasonable levels, tracking the rise of cost of living (the inflation index) and population growth. That was not the case, however, when George W. Bush was governor. Then, state spending grew far faster than inflation and population growth. Nor is that the case in many other states, which kept milking the cow of the productive private sector by imposing higher and higher taxes and spending more and more of the taxpayers' money. Those high-tax states are feeling the pain, as companies and taxpayers, suffering from high taxes and the loss of good jobs, move elsewhere. Moreover, the drop in housing prices and the slowdown in the economy since 2007 means that many states are racking up even more debt to fund state government.

Even in an ostensibly low-tax state like Texas, many local taxing bodies have shown little fiscal restraint in recent years. The housing boom allowed many of these local governments to raise property taxes in a seemingly painless fashion through the "stealth tax" of skyrocketing appraisal values. Property-tax revenues rose ten percent or more annually without local governments actually raising the tax rate. Local officials could tell voters that they had not raised taxes since the tax rate hadn't gone up, yet property-tax revenue grew from $9 billion in 1985 to $30 billion in 2004. That was approximately three times faster than the rate of inflation during the same period. Texas had the ninth-highest property taxes in the country until Governor Perry and the Texas legislature cut school property taxes by one third in 2006. Unfortunately, that set off a feeding frenzy among local taxing bodies, and a major portion of the education property tax cut was negated over the next three years.

When the Texas Task Force on Appraisal Reform (which I chaired at Governor Perry's request) sought to implement reforms to rein in these excessive property-tax hikes, lobbyists for the local taxing bodies killed our proposals in the 2007 regular session of the Texas legislature. Many of those local elected officials (and the career bureaucracy that runs local government) wanted no controls placed on their ability to spend as much of that "other people's money" as they could get their hands on. The local taxing bodies even used our own tax dollars to lobby against our proposals for property-tax relief and appraisal reform. Local and state governments regularly pay lobbyists to persuade state and federal governments to spend more tax dollars on projects benefiting their taxing entity. One well-connected transportation lobbyist from my home city of Dallas is paid $450,000 annually by local governments to get legislation passed that will help these localities pull down more transportation funding from the state and federal governments. In fact, the Republican legislator who led the effort to kill appraisal and property-tax reform in 2007 was hired by local taxing bodies to lobby for their interests in our state capitol after he retired from the legislature in 2008. Former state representative Fred Hill is now paid hundreds of thousands of dollars by local governments to block property-tax and appraisal reform in Texas.

The system is out of control.

Unfunded pension liabilities at the local and state levels present another huge problem that most Americans do not even know exists. Shad Rowe, the former chairman of the Texas Pension Review Board, calls it a "time bomb." The people who should care are taxpayers, "but they don't know anything about it," Mr. Rowe said in an interview with the *Dallas Morning News*. A report released in March 2009 revealed that the Texas Teachers Retirement Fund had unfunded liabilities of more than $40 billion as a result of the stock-market and hedge-fund collapse of 2008.

Economist Carl Pellegrini notes that the Michigan Public School Employee retirement system has $22 billion in unfunded pension and retirement medical liabilities. Huntington, West Virginia, spent about 20 percent of its city budget on pensions in 2008, or $7.5 million. According to the *Charleston Herald-Dispatch*, Huntington's firefighter's pension fund had assets to cover only three percent of its potential claims. The police pension fund was not in much better shape, at only nine percent funded. Unless the taxpayers of the state of West Virginia bail it out soon, West

Virginia state senator Bob Plymate said in early 2008, the city of Huntington may have to declare bankruptcy.

Here in Texas, the Employees Retirement Fund of Fort Worth had more than a $400 million shortfall in early 2007. The states of New Jersey and Illinois have huge shortfalls in their pension plans—at least $18 billion in New Jersey and $46 billion in Illinois. A U.S. Senate Finance Committee report in early 2008 noted that a growing number of state pension funds are less than 80-percent funded.

Warren Buffett warned of the looming public-pension crisis in his annual report to Berkshire Hathaway shareholders in 2008:

> Public pension promises are huge and, in many cases, funding is woefully inadequate. Because the fuse on this time bomb is long, politicians flinch from inflicting tax pain, given that problems will only become apparent long after these officials have departed. Promises involving very early retirement—sometimes to those in their low 40s—and generous cost-of-living adjustments are easy for these officials to make. In a world where people are living longer and inflation is certain, those promises will be anything but easy to keep.

The situation got much worse in 2008 and 2009 when the economic bubble burst and the stock market collapsed. Where is the money going to come from to make good on these unfunded pension liabilities?

In an interview with the *Financial Times* in August 2007, the comptroller general of the United States, David Walker, drew parallels between America's current fiscal irresponsibility and the fall of the Roman Empire:

> Mr. Walker warned that there were "striking similarities" between America's current situation and the factors that brought down Rome, including "declining moral values and political civility at home, an over-confident and over-extended military in foreign lands and fiscal irresponsibility by the central government."

"Sound familiar?" Mr. Walker said. "In my view, it's the time to learn from history and take steps to ensure the American Republic is the first to stand the test of time."

Walker argued that the fiscal imbalance in this country meant that the United States is "on a path toward an explosion." The big-government conservatism of the Bush administration has made a bad situation even worse. To get spending under control, it will take either a serious economic crisis to wake us up or sound-thinking elected officials at every level of government, who treat taxpayers' money as they would treat their own. The economic crisis hit our nation with the force of a hurricane in 2008. Yet our elected and appointed "leaders" in Washington, D.C., seem intent on solving the problems of spending and credit excess with larger doses of the same medicine.

Our motto needs to be, "Let's do more with less."

The Neoconservative Conquest of

American Foreign Policy

"Dulce bellum inexpertis."
("War is delightful to those who have no experience of it.")
~Erasmus

Americans generally have been wary of involvement in foreign wars. Our first president, George Washington, warned of the perils of "foreign entanglements" in his Farewell Address. The United States has traditionally followed a strategy of deterrence, regarding war as a remedy of last resort. We have tended to be cognizant of Christ's words in the Garden of Gethsemane: "He who lives by the sword shall die by the sword."

In World War I, World War II, the Korean War, the Vietnam War, and the Persian Gulf War, we came to the defense of allies under attack. One can question the wisdom of involving ourselves in any, or all, of those foreign conflicts; but one can make a strong case that each of those military interventions was justified from a moral standpoint. The same can be said for our reaction to the Osama bin Laden-directed attacks against innocent American civilians on September 11, 2001. By the standards of just-war theory, and as part of an overall strategy to deter the influence of militant Islam, we made the right decision to deny Osama bin Laden and his Taliban allies the sanctuaries in Afghanistan where they were training their radical followers in the techniques of sabotage and terrorism. U.S. support for the Northern Alliance and other anti-Taliban forces in their campaign to overthrow the Taliban regime was an honorable response to the suicide attacks of September 11.

In the wake of those attacks, not only did most of the rest of the world — with the exception of Muslim extremists — express sympathy with America for what we had been subjected to, but most nations were broadly supportive of American-led efforts to go after Osama bin Laden and the other perpetrators of these atrocities. The French newspaper *Le Monde* even declared, "We are all Americans now." That positive worldwide reaction translated into military and political support from our European allies as we sought to oust the Taliban from power in Afghanistan and to deprive Bin Laden's forces of their training camps and sanctuaries.

Had we continued to develop a strategy to marginalize and isolate Osama bin Laden, Al Qaeda, and the forces of radical Islam, the threat of militant Islam to the Western world would be far less pronounced than it is today.

The neoconservatives, however, were so obsessed with accomplishing their long-standing objective of ousting Saddam Hussein from power that they lost sight of the more important goal. Moreover, they were now well positioned both within and outside the Bush administration to persuade the President and the American public of the necessity of launching a preemptive war in Iraq.

Their campaign for a war in Iraq did not suddenly appear after September 11. Neoconservative ideologues had been arguing for the overthrow of Saddam Hussein ever since George H.W. Bush allowed the bloody, secular dictator to remain in power after allied forces drove the Iraqi military out of Kuwait in the Gulf War. In 1996, leading neoconservative advisors to Israeli Likud Party leader Benjamin Netanyahu coauthored a paper for the incoming Netanyahu government entitled "A Clean Break: A New Strategy for Securing the Realm." It called for the removal of Saddam Hussein from power in Iraq and the replacement of the Syrian regime. Among the Americans involved in preparing the report were Richard Perle, chairman of the Defense Policy Board Advisory Committee from 2001 to 2003; Douglas Feith, Undersecretary of Defense for Policy from 2001 to 2005 and the Director of the Office of Special Plans (OSP) at the Pentagon; and David Wurmser, an Israeli-American with dual citizenship who was a special assistant to John Bolton at the State Department until 2003, when he was appointed Mideast advisor to Vice President Dick Cheney.

In the spring of 1997, Bill Kristol established his Project for the

New American Century, which got the drumbeats going in conservative and Republican circles for military action to overthrow Saddam Hussein. The executive director of that Kristol initiative was Gary Schmitt, who had served as the executive director of the president's Foreign Intelligence Advisory Board from 1984 to 1988.

In 1998 Kristol's organization sent an open letter to President William J. Clinton, calling for military action to overthrow Hussein. The letter read in part:

> The only acceptable strategy is one that eliminates the possibility that Iraq will be able to use or threaten to use weapons of mass destruction. In the near term, this means a willingness to undertake military action as diplomacy is clearly failing. In the long term, it means removing Saddam Hussein and his regime from power. That now needs to become the aim of American foreign policy.

Among the prominent neoconservatives who signed the letter were Kristol and Schmitt, Bill Bennett, Paul Wolfowitz, James Woolsey, John Bolton, Robert Kagan, Elliott Abrams, and Richard Perle.

The Kristol propaganda machine for a policy of military intervention in the Middle East had received a huge boost in 1995 when Kristol persuaded media magnate Rupert Murdoch to provide extensive subsidies for Kristol's new opinion magazine, *The Weekly Standard*.

In the battle for the Republican presidential nomination in 2000, most of the neoconservative leaders—including Bill Kristol—supported John McCain rather than George W. Bush. With the election of George W. Bush to the White House, it appeared that the neoconservatives would not have much more influence over American foreign policy than they had in his father's administration.

Certain events, however, combined to put the former liberal Democrats, now known as neoconservatives, in control of American foreign policy during the George W. Bush presidency.

Unlike his father, who was very knowledgeable concerning foreign policy, George W. Bush was almost a blank slate when it came to international affairs. The younger Bush had rarely traveled abroad and had exhibited little interest in foreign policy, including while he was governor of Texas. The one major pre-election trip he made to the Middle East turned out to have a significant impact on his views regarding the Israeli-Palestinian conflict. While Palestinian leader Yasser Arafat snubbed Bush (a huge mistake, given the personality of the man who would be the next president of the United States), Israeli leader Ariel Sharon went out of his way to court him. That paid major dividends when Sharon and the Israeli government later attempted to persuade the inexperienced President fully to support Israel's major policy positions in the Middle East. The one-sidedness of George W. Bush's Middle East policy became so obvious that Brent Scowcroft, who had served as national-security advisor to President George H.W. Bush and who was chairman of George W. Bush's Foreign Intelligence Advisory Council Board, was quoted in the *Financial Times* as saying, "Sharon is the puppeteer, and Bush is the puppet." Scowcroft, a critic of the war in Iraq, lost his chairmanship soon thereafter.

Another factor contributing to the neoconservative conquest of foreign policy during the Bush administration was the selection of Paul Wolfowitz as a major foreign-policy advisor to candidate Bush in the 2000 presidential campaign. Even though Condoleezza Rice ostensibly was Bush's principal foreign-policy advisor, Wolfowitz overshadowed Rice. Wolfowitz's experience in the Reagan and George H.W. Bush administrations, his close ties to Dick Cheney, and his superior intellect led to his emergence as Bush's most influential advisor on international affairs. To cite just one example of that influence: Bush, like most Republicans, had been opposed to the Clinton administration's military intervention on behalf of the Islamic Kosovo Liberation Army against the Christian Serbs. During his presidential campaign, however, he reversed himself, reportedly on the advice of Wolfowitz.

The most important reason why the neoconservative faction became so influential during the Bush administration, however, was Bush's selection of Dick Cheney to be his vice-presidential running mate. Just as Ronald Reagan's selection of Bush's father in 1980 proved a fateful decision for the future of the conservative movement, the choice of Cheney had a huge impact on American conservatism, the Republican Party, and our country.

As Vice President, Dick Cheney became the *de facto* president of foreign policy during Bush's first term. Cheney was the "godfather" and protector of a slew of neoconservative foreign-policy advisors who were in key positions, not just on the Vice President's staff but throughout the Bush administration, to influence foreign policy.

It was a surprise to many longtime Republican activists (myself included) that a Ford Republican like Cheney had become so closely aligned to the neoconservative worldview. I have yet to see a definitive explanation of why and how that happened. Cheney's wife, Lynn (a student of public policy in her own right), has long been associated with the neoconservative movement. Gertrude Himmelfarb, the wife of neoconservative godfather Irving Kristol, went out of her way to cultivate Lynn Cheney when the two served together at the National Endowment for the Humanities (NEH). Mrs. Cheney was chairman of NEH from 1983 to 1993. Since the 1990's, she has been an adjunct fellow at the American Enterprise Institute (AEI), the leading neoconservative think tank in Washington, D.C. Dick Cheney himself has been a strong supporter of AEI's policy objectives, even serving on AEI's board of trustees (1997-99).

Whatever the reasons a longtime centrist Republican would turn into a neoconservative hawk, the man with the most influence over foreign policy in the Bush administration was fully in sync with the neoconservative advocates of a preemptive war in Iraq. Cheney was surrounded by neoconservative ideologues, beginning with his chief of staff, Lewis "Scooter" Libby. Before joining Cheney's staff, Libby had been the attorney for convicted international financier Marc Rich and helped Rich obtain a pardon from President Clinton.

The Vice President also placed a number of his neoconservative allies on the staff of National Security Advisor Condoleezza Rice.

Paul Wolfowitz was named deputy secretary of the Department of Defense, where he became the principal architect of the war in Iraq. Douglas Feith, a close ally of Wolfowitz, became the number-three man at defense as the undersecretary for policy. Feith established his own intelligence unit within his division, which became a very useful tool for the proponents of a preemptive war in Iraq. That Douglas Feith was placed in such a sensitive position in the first place was surprising since he had been the subject of an intelligence investigation when he served on the National Security Council (NSC) under Richard Allen during Reagan's first term.

When William Clark took over as director of the NSC from Allen, he let Feith go, reportedly because of his concerns that Feith had suspicious ties to a foreign power. Feith's career was salvaged when Richard Perle put him on his staff over at the Department of Defense.

A highly placed source in the Pentagon told me that certain circles in the Department of Defense had grave concerns about security-clearance issues when Wolfowitz pushed aggressively in 2001 to bring Douglas Feith into such a key position.

John Bolton, a longtime ally of the neoconservatives dating back to his service in the Reagan administration (where I first met him), was named Undersecretary of State for Arms Control and International Security. Bolton had been one of the signers of the 1998 letter to President Clinton, orchestrated by Bill Kristol's Project for the New American Century, calling for the overthrow of Saddam Hussein. Bolton had previously served as senior vice president of the American Enterprise Institute.

Bolton was Cheney's man at the Department of State. He was placed there in spite of reservations Secretary of State Colin Powell and his top advisors had about Bolton's close ties to the neoconservatives. Secretary Powell, Deputy Secretary Richard Armitage, and Powell's Chief of Staff Lawrence Wilkerson all had served as officers in Vietnam. They were very skeptical of the neoconservative goal of using U.S. military power to impose Western-style democracies in the Middle East. Wilkerson, in an interview with the *New York Observer* after he had left the Bush administration, made it clear how Powell and his team viewed Bolton: "The Vice President's spy in the State Department was Under-Secretary Bolton."

Like Cheney, John Bolton had managed to avoid military service in Vietnam. In Bolton's case, he joined the Maryland Army National Guard and openly declared why in his Yale 25th reunion book: "I confess I had no desire to die in a Southeast Asian rice paddy." Yet Bolton was not so reluctant to send other young Americans off to war in Iraq and to seek to expand the war to Iran.

From their positions of power in the George W. Bush administration, the neoconservatives were well placed to achieve their goal of toppling Saddam Hussein. September 11 gave them the ammunition they needed, even over the objections of Powell's team at state, CIA analysts, and experienced military leaders like generals Anthony Zinni and Norman Schwarzkopf who were opposed to a preemptive war in Iraq. As Paul Pillar notes in the March/April 2008 issue of *Foreign Affairs*, the intelligence community "anticipated the civil strife, terrorism, and instability that ensued."

That didn't stop the neocons.

Immediately after September 11, Paul Wolfowitz began to push the Bush administration to go to war in Iraq, even though the attacks had been directed by Osama bin Laden, not Saddam Hussein. George Tenet, then director of the CIA, claims that Richard Perle, who chaired President Bush's Defense Policy Board Advisory Committee from 2001 to 2003, made the case to him for targeting Iraq for military action. Neoconservative propaganda outlets began pushing the notion that Saddam Hussein was linked to Osama bin Laden and needed to be overthrown. Douglas Feith's newly created Office of Special Plans at the Department of Defense promoted the same line. The propaganda offensive was so successful that polls soon found over 50 percent of the American public thought that Saddam Hussein was responsible for September 11.

Nonetheless, the campaign to blame Hussein for September 11 proved insufficient to justify a preemptive war against Iraq. So the neoconservatives' next approach was to claim that Saddam Hussein had "weapons of mass destruction" (WMDs) that he would use against the United States unless we toppled him from power.

The WMD allegations resonated with an American public still in shock over September 11.

In an interview with *Vanity Fair* (July 2003) Deputy Secretary of Defense Paul Wolfowitz admitted that the WMD claim was just another ploy: "The truth is that for reasons that have a lot to do with the U.S. government bureaucracy, we settled on the one issue everyone could agree on which was weapons of mass destruction as the core reason" for going to war in Iraq.

In the intelligence business, we call it "cooking the books." I saw it firsthand as a military intelligence officer in Vietnam when there was a push to shape intelligence to fit the preconceived conclusions of the higher-ups. In the run-up to the war in Iraq, any information, no matter how dubious the source, supposedly connecting Saddam Hussein to Osama bin Laden was welcome in Douglas Feith's Office of Special Plans and publicly touted by neo-conservative advocates of the war. It didn't matter that Osama bin Laden and Saddam Hussein were bitter foes in the Arab world.

Any intelligence data supporting the charge that Saddam Hussein was developing WMDs was likewise highly prized, even if the information came from questionable sources. The claim that Hussein had attempted to acquire "yellowcake" uranium from Niger was the final piece of "evidence" that Vice President Cheney and his neoconservative allies inside the administration needed to get the President to set in motion the elimination of the Saddam Hussein regime and the "democratization" of the Middle East.

It turned out that this so-called smoking gun was an intelligence fabrication. In their book *The Italian Letter*, Peter Eisner and Knut Royce exposed the lie uttered by President Bush to justify going to war in Iraq: "The British government has learned that Saddam Hussein recently sought significant quantities of uranium from Africa." As Eisner and Royce prove, the entire claim was based on a bogus document.

The law of unintended consequences quickly came into play once we occupied Iraq. The war did not turn out like the neoconservatives told us it would, as these quotations collected by *The American Conservative* (May 5, 2008) show:

Richard Perle, chairman, Defense Policy Board (July 11, 2002): "Support for Saddam, including within his military organization, will collapse after the first whiff of gunpowder."

Richard Perle (July 11, 2002): "Now it isn't going to be over in 24 hours, but it isn't going to be months either."

Vice President Dick Cheney (August 26, 2002): "After liberation the streets of Basra and Baghdad are sure to erupt in joy."

Kenneth Adelman, member, Defense Policy Board (August 29, 2002): "Desert Storm II will be a walk in the park."

Michael Ledeen, Freedom Scholar, American Enterprise Institute (September 4, 2002): "If we come to Baghdad, Damascus and Tehran as liberators, we can expect overwhelming popular support."

Fouad Ajami, professor of Middle East studies, Johns Hopkins University (October 17, 2002): "We shall be greeted, I think, in Baghdad and Basra with kites and boom boxes."

Paul Wolfowitz, deputy secretary of defense (February 23, 2003): "You're going to find, and this is very important, you're going to find Iraqis out cheering American troops."

Richard Perle (September 22, 2003): "[A] year from now, I'll be very surprised if there is not some grand square in Baghdad that is named after President Bush. There is no doubt that, with the exception of a small number of people close to a vicious regime, the people of Iraq have been liberated and they understand they're liberated."

It should come as no surprise that the American people turned against the war once it was revealed that the neoconservatives had been as bad at predicting the outcome as they were at telling the truth.

Even before it became clear that the war would not be a "cakewalk," the neocons pushed the party line that the only critics of the war were "leftists." Conservative critics of the neoconservatives' Iraq obsession had to be silenced or discredited. Leading neoconservative David Frum was the perfect choice for hatchet man. Frum had earned his bona fides in neoconservative circles with a vicious personal attack against Pat Buchanan in the pages of *The American Spectator* in the early 1990's.

Frum recognized that many traditional conservatives—who had been around the movement a lot longer than he had—opposed the war from the beginning on solid, constitutional grounds and for sound strategic reasons. Among those Frum accused of being "unpatriotic conservatives" in his *National Review* cover story of the same name were conservative columnist Robert Novak, Pat Buchanan, the late Jude Wanniski (a leading theoretician of supply-side economics), Thomas Fleming (editor of *Chronicles: A Magazine of American Culture*), and Scott McConnell (editor of *The American Conservative*).

These and other conservative critics of the war were "exerting influence," Frum steamed. So he denounced them in a long and error-filled tirade in the pages of what had once been the leading voice of American conservatism. Frum ended his venomous piece with a warning to any conservative who dared to criticize our neoconservative-driven policy in the Middle East: "In a time of danger, they have turned their backs on their country. Now we turn our backs on them."

The irony is that this propagandist for the neoconservative party line on foreign policy who accused American opponents of the war in Iraq of being "unpatriotic conservatives" was never a true conservative in the first place. David Frum is an agnostic Canadian, a philosophical liberal at his core, with a barely disguised contempt for traditional-values conservatives.

Of course, conservative critics of the war have proved prescient. The war in Iraq has been extraordinarily expensive, both in human and economic terms. Approximately ten percent of our soldiers serving in Iraq have suffered casualties. The cost of the war to the American taxpayer will easily exceed a trillion dollars (and may go as high as three trillion dollars), with liabilities stretching far into the future. In light of our current economic troubles, it is worth recalling that one of Osama bin Laden's stated objectives was to drive the United States into bankruptcy by forcing us to spend large sums of money to respond to the September 11 attacks. The reality has undoubtedly exceeded his wildest dreams. After September 11, Bin Laden boasted that his operation against us had cost only half a million dollars. In the "War on Terror," the Bush administration spent hundreds of billions of dollars, and by the time the bills come due, that figure that will rise to several trillion.

As the effort to destroy Saddam's weapons of mass destruction proved fruitless (since they did not exist), the neocons redefined the goal of the war as "regime change" (which is what they wanted all along). Once Saddam Hussein was removed from power, however, the objective of the war became still more abstract. In an interview, President Bush assured the late Tim Russert that the regime that replaced Saddam would be democratic and secular, not religious, because Ahmed Chalabi, a notorious prevaricator who had received tens of millions of dollars from U.S. government sources over the years, had sat in the Oval Office and told him so. As the Iraqi regime became more demonstrably Islamic (and Shiite) in character, the stated objective of fostering pro-Western, democratic regimes in the Middle East was exposed as a fiction. The neocons were left with one last line of defense: It is better to fight the terrorists over there than to face them here at home.

Retired Air Force Intelligence Officer Steve Daskal puts all of this in proper perspective as he warns of the dangers of the neoconservative push to "export democracy" to the Middle East:

> I remain convinced that "democracy" as being promulgated around the world by American progressives/neoconservatives (and their European counterparts), is *not* conducive to creating limited, federal, pluralistic, market-oriented nations, but rather will lead to the rise of a variety of populist-dominated states that will have strong Islamist and/or fascist and/or Marxist-Leninist tendencies. What made the USA free and strong is not "democracy," but rather a limited, Constitutional, federal government with separation of powers, checks and balances, and a host of protections of individual rights against majority power and against the power of wealth or elected office. Democratic elections without all of those other structures and guarantees and without a solid Judeo-Christian and Common Law tradition, are not likely to enhance liberty much less establish it.

The neoconservatives' Wilsonian idea that Iraq would be the testing ground for Western-style democracy in the Middle East was fundamentally flawed. Iraq is still dangerous; the likelihood of a civil war breaking out once we leave remains strong; and life for Christians in Iraq is far worse today than it ever was. It is a lot harder to get our military forces in Iraq out of harm's way and to exit that situation honorably than it was to go into Iraq in the first place.

That is why we need the expert advice and guidance of retired military leaders like Gen. Anthony Zinni who understand the region well and can develop an appropriate exit strategy. It is too bad that General Zinni, who had been picked to be the U.S. ambassador to Iraq in the Obama administration, had his appointment blocked by powerful forces close to the President.

Not much media attention has been given to the plight of Iraqi Christians since the invasion. Christians have fared far worse under the U.S.-sponsored regime than they did when Saddam Hussein was in power. Under Saddam, Christians generally were left alone and allowed to practice their faith so long as they did not pose a political threat. Since the beginning of the war, Islamic factions have gained more influence and have taken their anger at the United States out on Iraqi Christians, who are leaving Iraq in droves. Chaldean Catholic Archbishop Louis Sako of Kirkuk, in northern Iraq, told AFP in October 2008 that Christians in Iraq "are the target of a campaign of liquidation, a campaign of violence. The objective is political." The archbishop pointed out that there were 800,000 Christians in Iraq at the time of the invasion; and, by the fall of 2008, one third of the Christians in Iraq had fled to other countries. He added, "The Christians of Iraq are not militias or tribes to defend themselves, we have a bitter feeling of injustice because innocent people are killed and we do not know why."

Gary Bauer and John Hagee—strong supporters of the war from the very beginning and closely aligned with the neoconservatives for many years—continue to promote the neoconservative party line in Iraq and elsewhere in the Middle East. Have Bauer and Hagee turned a blind eye to the dangers confronting their Christian brethren in Iraq and throughout the Middle East as a result of these misguided policies?

For Bauer and Hagee, destroying Iraq was not enough; both have demanded that we expand the war into Iran. In a well-received speech to the American Israel Public Affairs Committee in March 2007, Hagee, pastor of the Cornerstone Church of San Antonio, roared, "The ghost of Hitler is again walking across the stage of history. It is 1938; Iran is Germany and Ahmadinejad is the new Hitler."

Pastor Hagee believes that bombing Iran would be a fulfillment of biblical prophecy. Pastor Hagee has developed a significant following of "Christian Zionists" who maintain that we are near the "end times" and that the survival of the biblical Israel is central to the coming of Christ's Kingdom. U.S. policy in the Middle East, Hagee believes, should support without reservation the strategic interests of Israel, even if they may clash with our own national interests. Hagee's views echo the hawkish stance of the Netanyahu faction of the Likud Party, which has demanded the destruction of Iran's nuclear capability.

Pastor Hagee directly linked the destruction of Iran's nuclear program to Israel's survival in his AIPAC speech. "As you know," he said, "Iran poses a threat to the State of Israel that promises nothing less than a nuclear holocaust." "Ladies and gentlemen," he continued, "we must stop Iran's nuclear threat and stop it now and stand boldly with Israel, the only democracy in the Middle East."

Hagee's call for expanding the war in the Middle East is not based on his strategic assessment of Middle Eastern affairs but on his interpretation of certain language in the Bible—an interpretation that is at odds with the traditional Christian understanding of that same language. Nonetheless, in his AIPAC speech, Pastor Hagee maintained that tens of millions of evangelicals agree with him: "It's a new day in America. The sleeping giant of Christian Zionism has awakened; there are 50 million Christians standing up and applauding the State of Israel."

Since they emerged as a significant political force in the 1980 election between Ronald Reagan and Jimmy Carter, evangelical leaders have concentrated their attention on such social and cultural issues as abortion, homosexuality, "gay marriage," and pornography. Yet for Gary Bauer and John Hagee, where a presidential candidate stands on U.S. foreign policy in the Middle East has become a more important measure of whether he is deserving of their support. That unusual development within certain evangelical circles was amply demonstrated in the 2008 Republican presidential primary when Pastor Hagee and Gary Bauer supported Arizona Sen. John McCain against one of their own evangelical conservatives, former Arkansas governor Mike Huckabee. Before running for office, Huckabee had been a Baptist minister.

While McCain has been lukewarm in his support of cultural conservatism over the years, Huckabee has been a staunch supporter of pro-life and pro-family issues throughout his political career. Yet McCain was a down-the-line supporter of the neoconservatives' foreign policy, while Huckabee was considered "less reliable" on the use of U.S. military power to force democracy on the Middle East and thus viewed with suspicion in neoconservative circles.

The support of evangelicals such as Bauer and Hagee for their hawkish stance on Middle East policy is a significant reason why neoconservatives maintain a strong following in certain conservative circles, even after it has become clear that neoconservative-driven policy in the Middle East has been a disaster for Christians in the region and partly responsible for the Republican loss of the presidency and other political offices in 2008.

Nor is the news encouraging when one considers the effect the war in Iraq and its aftermath has had on our Armed Forces. The American military is badly overextended as it is forced to deal with insurgencies in Iraq and Afghanistan. Tours of duty of military personnel assigned to war zones are routinely extended without notice. Military reservists and national guardsmen made up more than 40 percent of our troops in Iraq even though the Reserves and the National Guard are not designed to dispatch large numbers of troops from their units for extended service in a foreign war zone.

Command Sgt. Major Neil Ciotola, a much-decorated Army officer who was Fort Hood's senior noncommissioned officer, told the Killeen, Texas, *Daily Herald* in mid-2008 that the soldiers are tired of fighting. "We, the Army, have been rode hard and put up wet. We're catching ourselves coming and going . . . In all honesty, ladies and gentlemen, I and the majority of us in uniform, and those that repeatedly support us, are tired." Our career soldiers, Sgt. Major Ciotola continued, "are tired, understaffed and under-equipped" after multiple deployments to the war zone.

As Andrew Bacevich, professor of international relations at Boston University and a former career military officer who served in Vietnam, pointed out: "Mr. Bush has too few soldiers doing too many things, while the rest of the country blissfully contents itself shopping and watching TV." In May 2007, Professor Bacevich's son was killed in action in Iraq.

Through our actions in the Middle East, we have set in motion a battle for political power among competing religious factions in the guise of democratic reform. As Leon Hadar points out,

> In reality, the local players, whether they are the Shiites and Kurds in Iraq or the Maronites, Druze, and Shiites in Lebanon, regard their partnership with a power like the United States as nothing more than an ad-hoc arrangement aimed at advancing their particular interests in relation to other competing players in the region.

As Thomas Ricks of the *Washington Post* told National Public Radio, the Shiite government of Iraq has come to consider American troops as "chumps," keeping the Shiites supplied with weapons while they wage war against the minority Sunnis.

In light of all of these problems, one would think that the neoconservative policy makers would be more cautious in advocating further U.S. military action in the Middle East. Yet leading neoconservative spokesmen continue to beat the drums for U.S. military action against the regimes in Syria and Iran. About the time that President Bush was making his "Mission Accomplished" speech on May 1, 2003, Bill Kristol was telling FOX News viewers that, since we had a victorious army in Iraq with nothing to do, we should send them into Syria. And Michael Ledeen, the Iran-Contra figure who is as enamored of Machiavelli as he is of American military might, constantly urges the United States to broaden the Middle Eastern conflict into Iran. Writing for *National Review Online*, Ledeen has ended countless articles with his mantra for action against Iran: "Faster, please!"

The neocons intend the United States to be the battering ram which imposes democracy by force throughout the Middle East.

71

Norman Podhoretz, a leading neoconservative commentator, refers to this process of "perpetual war" as "World War IV," the sequel to World War I, World War II, and the Cold War. Syndicated columnist Charles Krauthammer sees this as the logical consequence of America's "global dominion" as a new world empire:

> We have overwhelming global power. We are history's designated custodians of the international system. When the Soviet Union fell, something new was born, something utterly new—a unipolar world dominated by a single superpower unchecked by any rival and with decisive reach in every corner of the globe. This is a staggering new development in history, not seen since the fall of Rome. Even Rome is no model for what America is today.

Have we seriously considered the human and material costs to our nation of the pursuit of a foreign policy that seeks to impose our values on the rest of the world? Have we really understood the long-term consequences of the abandonment of our traditional view that American foreign policy should be guided by our national interest?

Paul Craig Roberts, a conservative columnist and former assistant secretary of the treasury in the Reagan administration, recognized the danger posed by the Iraq War early on. Roberts offered a blunt warning about the consequences of forsaking our national interest to impose our values on the rest of the world:

> Americans have been betrayed. Sooner or later, Americans will realize that they have been led to defeat in a pointless war by political leaders whom they inattentively trusted. They have been misinformed by a sycophantic corporate media too mindful of advertising revenues to risk reporting truths branded unpatriotic by the propagandistic slogan, "you are with us or against us."
>
> What happens when Americans wake up to their betrayal? It is too late to be rescued from catastrophe in Iraq, but perhaps if Americans can understand how such

a grand mistake was made they can avoid repeating it. In a forthcoming book from Oxford University Press, "The New American Militarism," Andrew J. Bacevich writes that we can avoid future disasters by understanding how our doctrines went wrong and by returning to the precepts laid down by our Founding Fathers, men of infinitely more wisdom than those currently holding reins of power.

Bacevich, a West Point graduate, Vietnam veteran and soldier for 23 years, is a true conservative. He is an expert on US military strategy and a professor at Boston University. He describes how civilian strategists—especially Albert Wohlstetter and Andrew Marshall—not military leaders, transformed a strategy of deterrence that regarded war as a last resort into a strategy of naked aggression. The resulting "marriage of a militaristic cast of mind with utopian ends" has "committed the United States to waging an open-ended war on a global scale."

The greatest threat to the United States is not terrorists but the neoconservative belief, to which President Bush is firmly committed, that American security and well-being depend on U.S. global hegemony and impressing U.S. values on the rest of the world.

The neoconservative goal of imposing democracy everywhere is the kind of utopian vision one generally associates with the left. It is akin to the Marxist objective of creating a "perfect world," a "heaven on earth." Conservatives generally are wary of utopianism. They understand the imperfectibility of man and our fallen nature. They are skeptical of man-made schemes to transform human nature—especially when they require abandoning our constitutional limits on power, as well as "the Laws of Nature and of Nature's God" that the Declaration of Independence points to as the foundation of our liberties.

There is a reason this utopian vision sounds leftist: The neoconservatives are not really conservatives at all, but liberals masquerading as conservatives. Moreover, as far as I have been able to determine, not a one of the neocon insiders driving our policy in the Middle East from 2001 on ever served in Vietnam, and only a few served in the military at all during that war, in spite of the fact that most of them were of draft-eligible age.

Of course, neoconservative and neoliberal demands for U.S. military intervention to impose our values on other parts of the world did not begin with the George W. Bush administration. A coalition of neoliberals and neoconservatives supported Bill Clinton in 1999 when he intervened militarily on behalf of the Kosovo Liberation Army (KLA). By and large, conservatives opposed the bombing of Serbia, which ultimately led to the control of Kosovo shifting from the Christian Serbs to the radical Islamic KLA. As Srdja Trifkovic has noted, Kosovo "was the birthplace of the Serbian state and the cradle of its culture." Trifkovic bluntly describes the consequences of this shift in power in an article entitled "The Poisoned Fruits of Clinton's War":

> In the aftermath of the bombing . . . and with tens of thou-
> sands of NATO soldiers occupying Kosovo, we've had mas-
> sive destruction of the priceless Serbian mediaeval heritage
> in the province, we've had wanton murders of hundreds of
> Serbs and other non-Albanian civilians in the province, and
> wholesale ethnic cleansing of the Serbs resulting in their
> near-disappearance from their ancestral lands.

Many conservatives at the time were critical of Clinton's bombing of Serbia. That was not the case, however, with Paul Wolfowitz, who persuaded then-candidate George W. Bush to support the war against Serbia. Neoconservatives, in seeming lockstep with the Madeline Albright neoliberal crowd, endorsed Clinton's military intervention in the Balkans. As conservative spokesmen Paul Weyrich and William Lind noted at the time, "With American aid, two new Islamic states have been created in the Balkans, Bosnia and Kosovo."

Yet the neoconservatives have yet to acknowledge that they were wrong to support a policy that has created a power base for radical Islam in the Balkans.

How is it in America's national interest to prop up and protect a militant Islamic state in the heart of Central Europe?

Neoconservatives are just as wrong when it comes to their support for Islamic radicals fighting against the Russians in the war in Chechnya. Richard Perle, Elliott Abrams, Kenneth Adelman, Midge Decter, Frank Gaffney, Michael Ledeen, Norman Podhoretz, Joshua Muravchik, Morton Abramowitz, Richard Pipes, Robert Kagan, and William Kristol have all joined in support of what they call a Chechen "movement of national liberation."

Of that insurgency, Paul Weyrich and William Lind, writing in 1999, noted:

> The current fighting in Chechnya began when Chechen Islamic militants attacked Russian Dagestan. In strategic terms, Russia's war is defensive. America's foreign policy establishment turns a willful blind eye to the Islamic danger. Having bombed the Christian Serbs out of their historic homeland of Kosovo, it is now denouncing Russia's counteroffensive in Chechnya. If we can prevent the Washington elite from stabbing Russia in the back and giving Islam yet another victory, we will have helped both Russian Christians and ourselves.

After September 11, the U.S. ambassador to Russia, Alexander Vershbow, stated that the United States "has long recognized that Osama bin Laden and other international networks have been fueling the flames in Chechnya." But, as Srdja Trifkovic pointed out in a special report for The Rockford Institute, weeks later Vershbow was instructed to say that the United States continued to oppose Russian policies in Chechnya. No wonder Russian President Vladimir Putin warned in late 2001 that "double standards" in the international fight against terrorism could split the global coalition: "There cannot be good and bad terrorists, our terrorists and others."

In the strategic struggle against militant Islam, Russia, Serbia, and other European nations need to be our allies, not our foes. It makes one wonder if neoconservatives hold more grievances against the Russians and Serbs than against the Islamic radicals, clouding their judgment as we attempt to develop an effective strategy against the spread of radical Islam in Europe.

Unfortunately, much of this information has not reached the American public. Through their control of the conservative media, the neoconservatives present only one "conservative" viewpoint on the threat of militant Islam to the American public, and thus what most Americans think of as American foreign policy today is really neoconservative ideology.

Conservatives must not continue to acquiesce to the flawed policies of these neoconservative "experts" who have gotten us into such a mess in the Middle East. Neoconservative policies have radicalized Muslim believers around the globe and alienated us from would-be allies who are just as threatened as we are by the rise of militant Islam.

We must quit listening to these liberal Democrats-turned-Republicans who remind me so much of the McNamara whiz kids in their abstract intellectualism. They may have high IQs, but much of what they "know" is not true. McNamara and his entourage pursued a failed strategy to combat the communist threat in Southeast Asia. With a similar "arrogance of intellect," neoconservative strategists have led us into a quagmire in the Middle East.

The worst of the lot is Paul Wolfowitz—the Robert McNamara of the Bush administration. Wolfowitz predicted before the war that "the U.S. would be treated as liberators, that Iraqi oil money would pay for the reconstruction, and that Gen. Eric Shinseki's estimate that several hundred thousand troops would be needed was 'widely off the mark.'" He was wrong on every issue. And he even acknowledged that the alleged basis for going to war, "weapons of mass destruction," was settled on for p.r. reasons.

True conservatives find themselves confused and divided. We are patriotic and want to support our soldiers. Like most Americans, conservatives were justifiably angry over the September 11 terrorist attacks and wanted to strike back at the enemy. But the neocon strategy of perpetual war in the Middle East is simply fanning the flames of militant Islam. We run the risk of destabilizing the Middle East and turning more Muslims into Al Qaeda supporters.

Michael Scheuer, the ex-CIA analyst who was in charge of going after Bin Laden at the agency, explains in *Imperial Hubris* why we are losing the War on Terror:

> As I complete this book, U.S., British, and other coalition
> forces are trying to govern apparently ungovernable postwar
> states in Afghanistan and Iraq, while simultaneously fighting
> growing Islamist insurgencies in each—a state of affairs our
> leaders call victory. In conducting these activities, and the
> conventional military campaigns preceding them, U.S. forces
> and policies are completing the radicalization of the Islamic
> world, something Osama bin Laden has been trying to do
> with substantial but incomplete success since the early 1990s.
> As a result, I think it fair to conclude that the United States of
> America remains bin Laden's only indispensable ally.

Unless the United States rejects these endless wars and re-establishes a foreign policy guided by our national interest, then the strategic threat of militant Islam will grow stronger. The "guns and butter" attitude toward spending by the Bush administration (eerily reminiscent of Lyndon Johnson's policies during the Vietnam War) will have long-term negative consequences for the American economy. The U.S. military, already stretched too thin, will suffer serious recruitment, morale, and leadership problems and will be unable to respond effectively when an unexpected crisis requires a U.S. reaction. Our concentration on military action in the Middle East and Afghanistan will cause us to neglect a serious cancer growing south of the border, where a communist regime headed by Hugo Chavez in Venezuela is seeking to extend its tentacles throughout South America. Already, leftists have made significant headway in Brazil, Argentina, Uruguay, Bolivia, and Peru. And the "open borders" policy of both the Bush and Obama administrations will be exploited by our enemies to wreak further havoc on our shores.

It is not too late to change course, but conservatives have to be willing to challenge publicly those who, in the name of conservatism, are leading this nation down the road previously traveled by the once-powerful Roman and British empires.

The Bubble Economy and the
Destruction of the Middle Class

"If I mistake not, the distress of the year 1857 was produced
by an enemy more formidable than hostile armies;
by a pestilence more deadly than fever or plague;
by a visitation more destructive than the frosts of
Spring or the blights of Summer. I believe that it
was caused by a mountain load of DEBT."
~Edward Everett, *Mount Vernon Papers*

The American economy once encouraged savings and invest-ment, but now it rewards investment bankers and private eq-uity funds for loading up companies with high levels of corporate debt. What has happened? How did we go from a system which emphasized the importance of thrift (and the building up of equity in one's home) to an economic climate that encourages individuals to borrow like there's no tomorrow? A nation that once took pride in producing trade surpluses and balanced budgets now is drown-ing in unsustainable levels of trade deficits ($857 billion in 2006) and huge budget deficits, nearly $2 trillion in FY 2010.

The American economy once was driven primarily by Main Street (manufacturing companies, small business entrepreneurs, and a thriving middle class); now, it is dominated by Wall Street financiers, investment bankers, and financial engineers. A country that prided herself on her strong manufacturing base, which pro-duced good-paying jobs for American workers, has morphed into an economic system in which American jobs are "outsourced" over-seas, our manufacturing base has been hollowed out, and middle-class Americans find themselves sliding downward economically—all in the name of globalization and "free trade." The rich are getting richer, and the middle class is becoming poorer, in a society where CEOs make 262 times the pay of the average worker.

What kind of economic future are we leaving for our children and grandchildren? The results of our "debtor society" are already evident in the case of young Americans coming out of our colleges and graduate schools. Too many young people find themselves saddled with massive student-loan debts before they even begin their careers. These financial obligations (some of which are in the six-figure range) may take decades to pay off. And still the cost of higher education grows far faster than inflation.

Equally disturbing in the new American economy is the loss of any ethical compass in the business world. Of course, there have always been rogues and crooks in American business who were willing to use shortcuts and to cheat to achieve financial advantage. I use the phrase "short around the corners" to describe business-men of this ilk for whom the end justifies the means. But their number is vastly increased these days.

Maybe it sounds a little hokey, but that old Texas expression about doing business on a handshake where "your word is your bond" still has relevance today in a corporate environment where the term "business ethics" has almost become an oxymoron. A business environment shaped by the Social Darwinist ethic of the "survival of the fittest" is as detrimental to the long-term viability of a free society as is the abrogation of property rights and the destruction of moral limits in the culture.

In the 1920's, before the Great Depression, Greenwich, Connecticut, was known as the richest town per capita in the world. With a plethora of hedge-fund managers located in Green-wich these days, it is one of the richest communities in the world once again (or at least it was until the credit bubble burst in 2008). As *Vanity Fair* reported, "Of the $1.2 trillion currently invested in hedge funds worldwide, approximately one-tenth, or $120 billion is now managed out of Greenwich alone, according to Hedge Fund Research, Inc. . . . To put that figure into perspective you should understand how small Greenwich really is: there are only about 23,000 households, a total population of 63,000."

To borrow a phrase from the novelist Tom Wolfe, hedge-fund managers in Greenwich, Connecticut, had become the new

"Masters of the Universe"—until the economic crash.

The dirty little secret in the hedge-fund world is the "2 and 20 rule." Hedge-fund managers take 2 percent of the funds invested as a "management fee" and a minimum 20 percent of the winnings. (Some private equity funds take even more.) At the same time, few fund managers give back to their investors out of their previous winnings 20 percent of any losses they incur if they have a bad investment year. Most fund managers win no matter what happens to their portfolio over the long term. So long as they have a couple of good years, in which they make 20 percent or more of the profits, they can set themselves up financially for the rest of their lives. Meanwhile, passive investors bear most if not all of the risk.

Thus the incentive for many fund managers is to maximize the gain in any particular year, because they get 20 percent of the upside while not having to worry about the downside (unless they have their own money invested in the fund).

Before the music stopped, Martin Wolf of the *Financial Times* warned about the inherent danger in this explosion of hedge funds. "The U.S. itself looks almost like a giant hedge fund," wrote Wolf. There are too many incentives to take on "under-appreciated risks" in order to garner big gains for the fund managers.

My old venture-capital boss Bill Bowen liked to say that the Wall Street crowd always finds new ways to separate Main Street Americans from their money. The hedge-fund craze is just the latest example of this phenomenon.

A favorite tactic of these "masters of the universe" is to get control of public or private companies, load them up with corporate debt, cut jobs, sell off assets, and declare a dividend which allows them to get some (or all) of their initial investment back. This allows them to play with "house money" rather than worry about losing their own funds.

The poster child for Wall Street greed is private-equity mogul Stephen Schwarzman, who took his private-equity firm public at just the right time in 2007 and cashed out to the tune of $677 million.

With the bursting of the Wall Street bubble in the fall of 2008, even Schwarzman took a financial hit, with his equity holdings in Blackstone Group losing much of their value. But he was well positioned to ride out the problems of our bubble economy. Schwarzman's compensation package from Blackstone for 2007 was more than $350 million, according to Elizabeth Lozarowitz of the *New York Daily News* (March 13, 2008). And that does not count the $677 million he took out of the company when Blackstone went public that year.

Obviously, Stephen Schwarzman is among the big winners in this new economy of ours. Wall Street financiers have replaced Main Street owners of businesses as the driving force in the American economy. In addition, many of the "managers" of our public companies seem to run their corporations more for their own benefit than for the shareholders whose interests they are supposed to represent.

Some have described this as "crony capitalism." The late Bill Thomas, an old-style venture capitalist from Dallas, Texas, called it "corrupting capitalism." There is nothing I can add to his strong words:

> For several years I have condemned the outrageous salaries, bonuses, stock options, stock grants, severance and retire-ment benefits and a long list of other give aways to the man-agers of our nation's major corporations. The stockholders' pockets are being picked again and again by greedy, self-serving CEOs aided and abetted by indifferent boards of di-rectors. These boards continue to ignore their fiduciary du-ties as they casually betray the stockholders they are elected to represent.
>
> Each year Forbes publishes the compensation including gains on exercise of stock options paid to the CEOs of our country's 500 largest corporations. The relentless climb in the outrageous transfer of wealth from corporations' own-ers to their managers has continued unabated over the past quarter century. In 2005, the median compensation of the highest paid 100 CEOs was $22,300,000—slightly below the previous year. But, the median compensation of all 500 was $5,520,000—17.7 percent above the previous year.
>
> Meanwhile, the Bureau of Labor Statistics reports that the average production worker earned $28,315 in 2005—an

increase of only 3.1 percent. How can we possibly condone a corrupt system that pays the median top 100 executives 788 times as much as the average worker or the median of the top 500 CEOs 195 times as much?

Then you have the old fashioned con men who took advantage of these "go-go" years to separate investors from their money. The most bizarre tale of recent Wall Street greed was the $50 billion Ponzi scheme run by "Wall Street Wizard" Bernard Madoff, whose fraud was successfully perpetrated on supposedly sophisticated investors and hedge-fund managers as well. The Texas billionaire "Sir" Alan Stanford had his own Ponzi formula for fleecing investors.

Pope Benedict XVI has warned of "the cynicism of a world without God, where only power and profit count." Is that what we are seeing in the raping and pillaging of public companies by corporate managers and private equity moguls, at the expense of employees and investors, for their own personal gain?

A central reason for those huge trade deficits and the shift of economic power from Main Street to Wall Street is a business tax system that gives private-equity moguls incentives to take such risks with the companies they control. In this respect, they have a distinct advantage over owners of U.S. companies who would like to run their businesses in a conservative fashion but find our tax structure onerous. The United States has a corporate income-tax rate of 35 percent. That rate is an economic incentive for financiers to load a company up with high levels of corporate debt in order to avoid taxation. It is a no-brainer—you can write off debt on your taxes, but savings and investments get taxed heavily. Why would any businessman want his company to accumulate significant savings if interest on those savings is taxed at 35 percent?

American businesses that have most of their plants and employees in the United States do not get to operate on a level playing field with our trading partners and competitors. Every major trading country in the world, except for the United States, provides a tax advantage for domestic manufacturers. As they have removed tariffs over the past four decades, they have put into place a value-added tax (VAT) that provides their companies with a significant economic advantage over foreign businesses.

Austin business economist David Hartman has developed some interesting data on the effects of a border-adjusted VAT.

Starting with France in the mid-1960's, European countries began adopting border-adjusted VATs that now average 19 percent. All OECD countries, other than the United States, have since adopted VATs or their equivalents averaging 18 percent. As a result, U.S. goods carry the full burden of federal, state, and local taxes, plus an added tax averaging 18 percent when they are shipped to foreign markets. To make matters worse, foreign goods that are shipped into the United States enjoy an 18-percent VAT abatement—yet are subject to none of the taxes imposed on U.S. manufacturers. Small wonder that General Electric increased "its manufacturing base outside the U.S. by nearly half" over just three years.

This horrendous inequity has turned the trade surplus that America once enjoyed into an abysmal trade deficit. Doug Ingram has called this "exporting prosperity."

Manufacturing jobs are not the only ones threatened by the new economy. Information-technology companies are in full-scale "outsourcing" mode. Numerous companies have moved their call centers to India and other foreign lands. When he ran for president in 1992, Ross Perot, the original founder of Dallas-based EDS, warned that the passage of the North American Free Trade Agreement (NAFTA) would mean a "giant sucking sound" as jobs headed south of the border. These days, EDS has shifted much of its workforce to India, and Perot Systems, where Ross Perot serves as chairman emeritus, has joined its competitors in outsourcing IT jobs to India and Mexico. In 2004, Perot Systems added 3,500 jobs to its India operations, on top of the 3,000 (out of 13,000 employees worldwide) who were already there. In 2006, Perot Systems opened a tech-services center in Guadalajara, Mexico.

When the subprime-mortgage bubble burst in 2007, sovereign-wealth funds from Asia and the Middle East began buying major stakes in U.S. financial institutions and other U.S. businesses. A poll by Public Strategies, Inc., reported in the *Wall Street Journal* (February 21, 2008), found that 56 percent of Americans opposed this partial sale of U.S. financial institutions to investment funds run by foreign governments, while only 8 percent favored it. The purchases were financed by our huge trade deficits. Of course, the foreign funds' timing was not particularly good, since many of our large financial institutions were practically broke. But dollar-rich foreign nations will continue to buy viable U.S. businesses for the foreseeable future.

In order to revitalize the American economy before it is too late, we have to address both structural and ethical problems.

Where do we begin?

Legendary investor Warren Buffett warned in a speech at the University of Nevada that "The U.S. trade deficit is a bigger threat to the domestic economy than either the federal budget deficit or consumer debt and could lead to 'political turmoil.'" Today, the rest of the world owns three trillion dollars more of us than we own of them.

Buffett warned that we run the risk of becoming a "Share-cropper's Society" rather than an "Ownership Society" if we do not address our huge trade deficits and the loss of our manufacturing base: "At this rate, the rest of the world will soon own our country. That's because we have to borrow from other countries to finance the trade deficit. We're mortgaging the farm an acre at a time."

Texas oilman and entrepreneur T. Boone Pickens points out the economic effect of our excessive dependence on foreign oil:

> Do you know how much oil we're buying, money going out
> of the country every year? Do you know what it's up to now.
> Half a trillion dollars a year. . . . We can't stand that. You take
> 10 years and you've got 5 trillion dollars, it's a huge change
> in the wealth . . . it's moving out of the States and into the
> hands of people, most of them we don't even know. And
> some of them are our enemies.

Both David Hartman and former assistant secretary of the treasury Paul Craig Roberts have warned of the consequences to our nation if we lose our manufacturing base. As Roberts wrote in a February 2006 column, "U.S. manufacturing lost 2.9 million jobs (over the last five years), almost 17 percent of the manufacturing workforce. The wipeout is across the board. Not a single manufacturing payroll classification created a single new job."

David Hartman reports that

Employment in manufacturing as a share of U.S. employment has fallen over 60 percent (since the 1950s), with a 20 percent decline just since 1998, the worst layoff since the Great Depression. The real average factory hourly wage, which traditionally had been the vanguard of "blue collar" compensation, declined 11 percent from 1978 to 2001.

The decline in the manufacturing sector increased during the eight years of the George W. Bush presidency. As Floyd Norris pointed out in the *New York Times* in February 2008,

The decline [in manufacturing jobs] in the current administration, at a rate of 3.1 percent a year, is the steepest yet seen.

When President Bush took office, nearly 13 percent of American jobs were in manufacturing. In November [2007], that figure fell below 10 percent for the first time ever; and at last measure was 9.95 percent.

Symbolic of the ongoing shift of American business away from the United States was the decision by General Electric to move many of its major business operations overseas. As reported in the *New York Times* (February 14, 2008), G.E. Healthcare moved from Wisconsin to England in 2004. The headquarters of the G.E. Money unit was moved from Stamford, Connecticut, to London in early 2008. G.E. previously had moved a major unit that sells equipment to energy companies to Florence, Italy. Halliburton, where Dick Cheney formerly served as CEO, moved its corporate headquarters from Houston, Texas, to Dubai in March 2007.

As Hartman notes, the continued disintegration of the U.S. manufacturing sector

threatens future progress and prosperity of the U.S. economy and loss of the most vital source of U.S. military security.

86

Manufacturing has perennially been the leading sector in the technological progress which drives productivity across all sectors of the U.S. economy and enables superiority of defensive weaponry. The accumulating obligation from massive trade deficits is irresponsible policy for a nation already facing unfunded multi-trillion dollar welfare obligations for "baby boom" retirees.

The late Dr. Kurt Richebächer observed that Washington policymakers and Wall Street economists have played down the negative effects of our unsustainable trade deficits in their determination to defend the principle of "free trade" at all costs:

One cannot say that U.S. policymakers and economists have been preoccupied with worries about possible harmful effects of the exploding trade deficit. They appear obsessed with the conventional wisdom that free trade is good and must always be good under any and all circumstances, as postulated in the early 19th century by David Ricardo.

Ricardo exemplified this by comparing trade in wine and cloth between Portugal and England. Portugal was cheaper in both products, but its comparative advantage was greater in wine. As a result, according to Ricardo, Portugal boosted its production and exports of wine. In contrast, England gave up its wine production and could produce more sophisticated goods. In both countries, living standards rose.

For sure, it appears highly plausible that American policymakers feel they are following Ricardo's logic. Only they are disregarding some caveats of Ricardo's. For equal benefit, first of all, balanced foreign trade is required. "Exports pay for imports" was a dogma of classical economic theory. Ricardo, furthermore, disapproved of foreign investment, with the argument that it slows down the home economy.

With an annual current account deficit of more than $800 billion, the U.S. economy is definitely a big loser in foreign trade. To offset this loss of domestic spending and income, alternative additional demand creation is needed. Essentially, all job losses are high-wage manufacturing, and most gains are in low-wage services. In essence, the U.S. economy is restructuring downward, while the Chinese economy is restructuring upward.

On another front, Americans have for years lived beyond their means and continue to accumulate unsustainable levels of debt. In a column in *Barron's* entitled "Spendthrift Nation," Alan Abelson notes that Americans had a negative savings rate in both 2005 and 2006. The last time we saw two consecutive years of negative savings was in 1932 and 1933, in the depths of the Great Depression.

Particularly affected by the negative savings rate are the poorer 50 percent of our population. Abelson quotes analyst Stephanie Pomboy: "The top 1% of households hold 30% of the assets and 7% of the debt, while the bottom 50% hold a mere 6% of the assets but a burdensome 24% of the debt."

In his weekly report of the state of the American economy, John Mauldin cites a study by Dennis Gartman about this shift toward negative savings. According to Gartman, savings rates across various categories of Americans were nearly 10 percent in 1991. They turned negative by 2000, when Americans with a home equity line of credit had a minus-9 percent savings rate. By 2005, that had turned into a minus-13 percent savings rate. As of 2007, the savings rate had returned to a less onerous minus-7 percent. Still, a shift from a positive 10 percent savings rate to a minus-7 percent one in a decade and a half is worrisome.

The consumer savings rate finally turned positive in 2008 and 2009 in the wake of the devastating national recession. Americans worried about keeping their jobs or making sure their businesses survived in difficult economic times suddenly started putting some money away for a rainy day.

Credit-card debt is wildly out of control. In 2006 I wrote about "the crazy credit card culture" and cited a story from *BusinessWeek* about a credit-card holder making $17,000 per year who had "maxed out" her $12,000 limit on one credit card. She applied for a second credit card and was approved—with another $12,000 line of credit. Needless to say, this story did not have a happy ending for either the borrower or the lender. Obviously, both parties are at fault. The debtor should never have paid for goods on credit which she had no ability to repay. At the same time, what kind of business extends a $12,000 line of credit to a person making $17,000 per year who already has a $12,000 unpaid obligation on another credit card?

The credit-card craziness in our society is matched by the "credit excess" in the residential-housing market. Housing prices in 2007 fell by nearly 8 percent, while new home sales fell by 26 percent, the steepest drop since records were first compiled in 1963. Some of us have been warning about this looming problem for years now. Writing in the *Dallas Morning News* (June 21, 2006), Danielle DiMartino pointed out "the vulnerability of so many young homeowners who've been hoodwinked by the lending community into borrowing more money to buy a home they cannot afford to pay back. Forty-two percent of those using ARMs are low income." (ARMs are adjustable-rate mortgages, which subject the borrower to significant increases in monthly payments when interest rates rise.)

I have used the phrase "passing the trash" to describe mortgage companies putting buyers into homes they cannot afford and then, after taking out their origination fees, passing the bad paper on to other investors. In October 2006, Bear Stearns' mortgage unit filed a lawsuit in U.S. district court in Dallas against MortgageIT Holdings, Inc., claiming that the company had passed on "bad mortgages that quickly defaulted." The *Wall Street Journal* reported that Bear Stearns was trying to force MortgageIT Holdings to buy back "at least 587 loans totaling $70 million."

"Who takes the hit when loans go bad?" the *Journal* asked. In days gone by, banks and savings and loans, which were responsible for most of the residential mortgages, were on the hook if they went bad. During the recent "go-go" years in the residential-mortgage market, a vast array of "exotic loans" were packaged and shipped out to Wall Street, where the loans were put into much larger packages. These included such risky loans as "no money down," "interest only" for an extended period of time, "no income verification," and adjustable-rate mortgages that started out at a low interest rate but could go a lot higher. Many of these loans were destined to go into default—which is precisely what they did, in massive numbers, beginning in 2007. Yet the signs of trouble were there years earlier for anyone paying attention to what was happening in the subprime market.

In March 2007, another disastrous case hit the news. The collapse of New Century Financial and a host of other subprime mortgage lenders is a telling indictment of those financial executives who tossed traditional lending standards out the window in their rush to make a quick buck.

New Century was an Irvine, California-based mortgage broker that specialized in making loans to buyers with questionable credit. The *New York Times* reported (March 5, 2007) that New Century would write loans to people "with low income and weak credit" and then sell them off to other lenders or investors as part of larger packages of collateralized mortgages. In other words, they would "pass the trash" after making their money on origination fees.

Just about any applicant, it appears, could get a home loan from New Century. For example, 42 percent of the loans they made in 2006 were either "stated income" or "interest only," according to *Forbes*. "Stated income" means that the borrowers do not have to provide any documentation to back up the income figure that they provide on their mortgage application—which is why these are often called "liar loans." "Interest only" home loans are usually a gamble that home prices will continue to appreciate.

The "passing the trash" business model was lucrative for executives and brokers. The *New York Times* story cites the case of Kal Elsayed, a former executive at New Century Financial. Elsayed acknowledged that "Driving a red convertible Ferrari to work at a company that provided home loans to people with low incomes and weak credit might have appeared ostentatious," but "that was nothing compared with the private jets that executives at other companies had."

"You just lost touch with reality after a while because that's just how people were living," said Mr. Elsayed, 42, who spent nine years at New Century before leaving to start his own mortgage firm in

2005. "We made so much money you couldn't believe it. And you didn't have to do anything. You just had to show up."

As the *Times* article pointed out, the subprime lending business "turned mortgage bankers and brokers into multi-millionaires seemingly overnight" while putting borrowers into homes with mortgages they could ill afford. This was the financial "gravy train" of the first decade of the 21st century. "[T]he three founders of New Century," the *Times* reported, "together made more than $40.5 million in profits from selling shares in the company from 2004 to 2006."

W. Scott Simon, a managing director at Pimco Advisors, summed up the subprime-mortgage industry well when he told the *New York Times*, "They walked into a niche industry at a time when everything was lining up perfectly for what they did. In 2001, 2002 and 2003, the sub-prime business was just phenomenally profitable. Home prices kept appreciating and it seemed that no loans ever went bad."

Chuck Prince, the former CEO of Citigroup, was asked by the *Financial Times* in 2007 about the economic bubble fueled by loose lending standards and excessive credit. His response: "So long as the music is playing, you've got to keep dancing." The music ended for Mr. Prince shortly thereafter, when the housing bubble burst.

The music stopped for a lot of companies that year. New Century Financial, whose stock was nearly $66 in December 2004, filed for bankruptcy protection in 2007. The Wall Street investment bank Bear Stearns, which was heavily invested in subprime paper, would have had to do the same in 2008 were it not for the taxpayer bailout of Wall Street, in which we paid JPMorgan Chase to take over the beleaguered investment bank.

Foreclosures reached 2.2 million in 2007, up 75 percent from 2006, while the median home sales price declined percentage-wise more than at any time in the previous 37 years. The foreclosure rate was nearly 1 in every 62 households—"a rate approaching heights not seen since the Great Depression," according to James Stack of InvesTech Research. Peer Steinbruk, the German finance minister, estimated in early 2008 that the subprime credit loss was heading toward $400 billion.

91

Among the biggest losers have been those unfortunate investors who wound up holding these questionable mortgages. But even more unfortunate are those of modest means who took out mortgages for which they would not have qualified had proper lending standards been followed. Many of these borrowers now find themselves "under water," owing much more on their house than it is currently worth. And, of course, the American taxpayer will wind up paying for the excesses of the Wall Street crowd.

In the 1980's, Texas went through a meltdown in the housing market that was aided and abetted by the "get rich quick" schemes of those who had gained control of many of the S&Ls and bled them for personal gain. We are now going through another mortgage meltdown. While the subprime-mortgage sector unraveled first, the effect quickly spread through our entire credit system. This time, the problem is not limited to the Southwest. This spells bad news for the American economy and numerous financial institutions. It also spells disaster for many homeowners who will pay a heavy price for getting sucked in by the "pass the trash" business model.

In the wake of the credit-fueled housing bust of 2007, one would have expected policymakers to address the serious problems facing the American economy today—a weak dollar, huge budget deficits, unsustainable trade deficits, out-of-control federal spending, and a business tax that penalizes savings and investment while rewarding debt. Instead, those directing economic policy have prescribed more of the same medicine that got us into this mess.

When the housing bubble burst, Fed Chairman Ben Bernanke did what his predecessor, Alan Greenspan, had done when the stock-market bubble burst in 2000: He cut interest rates dramatically. Within a two-week period in January 2008, the Fed cut rates from 4.5 percent to 3 percent. As I write, in mid-2009, Fed interest rates are virtually at zero.

In early 2008, with bipartisan support, the Bush administration got the Democratic-controlled Congress to pass a $168 billion package of tax rebates to individuals (including to people who had never paid taxes in the first place) in order to stimulate consumer spending.

The problem in the United States, however, is not a lack of "consumer demand." Rather, too many Americans have been living paycheck to paycheck, and setting very little aside for the future or for emergencies. Lack of savings and investment are the major reasons why the U.S. economy is ailing.

By lowering interest rates below the real rate of inflation, Fed Chairman Bernanke repeated Alan Greenspan's mistake. The Fed's 3 percent interest rate in January 2008 was well below the 4.3 percent Consumer Price Index (CPI) estimate of inflation. Such an artificially low rate of interest may be great for banks and for borrowers, but it is a lousy deal for savers, particularly those living on a fixed income who are dependent on their savings. Bush's "guns and butter" spending policies, combined with artificially low interest rates, are setting us up for a repeat of the stagflation of the 1970's.

We are passing out money we do not have through a Keynesian stimulus package designed to revive the economy. The same month the stimulus fix was announced, Moody's declared that the United States was at risk of losing its triple-A credit rating within a decade unless it addressed the federal government's "soaring" spending. One American economist bluntly stated that "the United States looks like an emerging market," with large deficits and a weak currency.

Our economic problems did not appear overnight. We cannot lay all of the fault at the feet of the Bush administration. Yet both the Clinton and the Bush administrations failed to address the underlying causes of the "bubble economy," preferring to keep the music playing while they were in power.

There is plenty of blame to go around—from Alan Greenspan to Ben Bernanke at the Federal Reserve, from Robert Rubin to Henry Paulson at Treasury, from Bill Clinton to George W. Bush in the White House.

In August 2002, I wrote an article for *ChroniclesMagazine.org* entitled "Toward a New Economic Policy." The arguments I made therein are just as valid today as they were then:

One of my favorite scenes in *Casablanca* is when the French Inspector, played by Claude Rains, is "shocked" to discover that gambling is going on in the back room of Rick's, a club owned by Humphrey Bogart, who plays an American expatriate in the film.

That scene comes to mind as I observe Washington politicians, Democrats and Republicans alike, try to outdo one another in expressing outrage over the corporate excesses that took place on Wall Street and in public companies during the stock market boom of the 1990's. During that speculative period, a number of Wall Street investment firms engaged in their time-honored custom of separating Main Street investors from their hard-earned money while certain corporate managers treated shareholder-owned public companies as though they were their own private fiefdoms. Since it was just "other people's money," the Wall Street hotshots and corporate insiders grabbed as much as they could as fast as they could—indifferent to the fact that the corporate and credit excesses fueling this boom would result in a very hard landing for investors and jeopardize the long-term viability of many of these companies.

A number of public figures now preaching "corporate reform" were right in there alongside the insiders grabbing their share of the loot, or helping to fuel a stock-market bubble which was bound to burst. Terry McAuliffe, Chairman of the Democratic National Committee, turned a $100,000 investment in Global Crossing into a $10 million windfall before that telecom debacle imploded. Senator John Corzine of New Jersey, whose Wall Street winnings at Goldman Sachs propelled him into a U.S. Senate seat in 2000, now advises his fellow Senate Democrats on how to reform corporate America. Yet, at Goldman Sachs, Corzine and his fellow executives couldn't push out the door fast enough to the investing public Initial Public Offerings (IPOs) of dubious dot-com and telecom companies with insignificant revenues and no history of profitability. Bill Clinton's Secretary of the Treasury, Robert Rubin, kept the credit bubble going in its early stages by bailing out the New York investment banks in the mid-90's when they got on the wrong side of the derivatives-trading market in the Mexican peso devaluation. That story is painstakingly told in the book *Fiasco* by Frank Partnoy, a former New York investment banker. Rubin later joined Citigroup which stands accused by congressional investigators of helping Enron hide debt through so-called structured financial instruments.

Lest I be accused of neglecting Republican complicity during this era of "crony capitalism," certain aspects of the Harken Energy and Texas Ranger transactions (which made George W. Bush a wealthy man) hardly pass the smell test. And Vice President Cheney has his own set of problems associated with accounting issues at Halliburton during his tenure as president of that company.

It makes one wonder why the public should have any confidence in the credibility of our political leaders to fix these corporate and credit excesses which didn't just appear overnight. It is not as though American investors weren't warned a few years ago about accounting problems, financial abuses, and credit excesses associated with many high-flying stocks. Astute financial analysts such as Dallas-based David Tice of the Prudent Bear Fund and noted short seller James Chanos warned of accounting problems at Tyco and Enron respectively long before those two stocks tanked. Tice and his associate Doug Noland preached repeatedly about credit excesses associated with the dot-com, telecom, and high-tech bubbles in the 90's. Now, they are telling investors to watch out for the housing bubble which they warn will be the next one to burst. Richard Russell, editor of the *Dow Theory Letter*, told investors as early as 1999 about the unsustainability of the bull market and said that we were heading into a secular bear market. Stephen Roach of Morgan Stanley has made a persuasive case for a double-dip recession and a declining value for our dollar in light of our huge account deficits.

Our economic woes won't be resolved by having more photo ops of corporate executives being carted off to jail. This may make irate investors somehow feel better about their losses and allow politicians to beat their breasts about how tough they are on these corporate "bad guys." But the market itself already is taking care of those companies which engaged in "creative accounting" by brutally punishing their stock prices.

Instead, what we need is a coherent economic policy which addresses our economic problems, particularly credit excess and malinvestment. In this regard the Fed policy of prolonging the housing bubble by keeping interest rates artificially low is not helpful. Nor does the federal government help to solve our problems by engaging in a spending binge at a time of declining tax revenues. Government at every level (just like the private sector) must figure out how to "do more with less" during this recessionary environment. We need to combine a fiscal policy which seeks to restrain government spending with a tax policy designed to encourage savings and capital investment.

Finally, the American public must understand that there is a heavy price to pay down the road for our unusually high levels of credit card and mortgage debt, especially if our economy doesn't rebound quickly. In spite of what we might wish, debt still doesn't go away any more than an "irrationally exuberant" stock market lasts forever.

There is always the temptation to resort to short-term solutions to serious problems so that bad things do not happen on your watch. Who wants to be thought of as the next Herbert Hoover?

But this refusal to face reality cannot go on forever. With budget deficits projected to be in the range of two trillion dollars for FY 2010, unsustainable trade deficits, and a national recession that could turn into a depression, we are setting ourselves up for a perfect storm of an economic disaster that could make Japan's economic woes of the 1990's look mild in comparison and even rival the Great Depression of the 1930's.

How do we deal with the consequences of the credit excess which fueled the stock-market bubble in the late 1990's and the housing bubble in this decade? We cannot undo the "sunk costs" of a flawed Fed policy engineered by Alan Greenspan and repeated by Ben Bernanke. As economist Steve Hanke points out, "things go wrong when a central bank sets short-term interest rates too low and allows credit to expand artificially. The result is an asset-price boom. Asset-price booms sow the seeds of their own destruction: They end in slumps." That is precisely where Greenspan's policy has led us. *The Economist* describes the result:

> The Fed held real interest rates negative for several years, and even today real rates remain low ... The Economist has long criticized Mr. Greenspan for not trying to restrain the stockmarket bubble in the late 1990s, and then, after it burst, for inflating a housing bubble by holding interest rates low for so long. The problem is not the rising asset prices themselves but rather their effect on the economy. By borrowing against capital gains on their homes, households have been able to consume more than they earn. Robust consumer spending has boosted GDP growth, but at the cost of a negative personal saving rate, a growing burden of household debt and a huge current-account deficit. ... Part of America's current prosperity is based not on genuine gains in income, nor on high productivity growth, but on borrowing from the future. The words of Ludwig von Mises, an Austrian economist of the early 20th century, nicely sum up the illusion: "It may sometimes be expedient for a man to heat the stove with his furniture. But he should not delude himself by believing that he has discovered a wonderful new method of heating his premises."

Now that the credit-fueled investment boom has ended, perhaps this will help slow down the credit-card excesses that have caused so many individuals and families to fall so heavily into debt. Doing something about what we used to call usury would also slam the door on these credit excesses.

The definition of usury is the practice of lending money and charging the borrower an exorbitant rate of interest. Such rates used to be illegal in most states in this country, but that is not the case anymore. A special law passed by Congress exempted most major financial institutions and credit-card companies from state usury limits.

One example of predatory lending at usurious rates of interest are the "payday lenders," many of whom have offices near military bases. As *Consumer Action* notes, "Payday lenders typically require borrowers to endorse a postdated check and then trap them into rolling the loan over repeatedly at annual percentage rates that can top 400 percent. The average payday borrower pays back $827 on a $339 loan."

Congress finally stepped in to protect our military personnel from these predatory lenders by capping the annual percentage rate to service members at 36 percent. Interest is defined to include all extra charges and fees of any kind, including the sale of related products like credit insurance. But that cap applies only to borrowers who are military personnel. It needs to apply to all borrowers.

Consumer credit cards also hook customers who do not pay off their obligations in a timely manner with interest, penalty, and fee charges that quickly rise to the level of usury. The "extra charges" are where the credit-card companies really sock it to consumers. A Supreme Court decision in 1978, the *Marquette Bank* opinion, allowed national banks to charge whatever interest rates were allowed in the state where their credit-card division was based, thus overriding usury laws in all 50 states. Citibank, whose credit-card business was struggling at the time, went to South Dakota and got the state legislature there to pass legislation eliminating its usury laws. Citibank promised it would send jobs to South Dakota in return. The rest is history. The "credit-card craze" was set to explode as companies could export their higher rates to other states and override any usury laws in place at the state level.

Andrew Kahr, one of the architects of the credit-card industry and founder of the company that became Providian, told *Frontline* that "It didn't require a lot of investigation to see that the people who paid in full every month were not profitable." The profitable ones were those "consumers who routinely carried high balances, but were unlikely to default."

Not only are those consumers saddled with high interest rates, which are clearly usurious under the traditional definition of the word *usury*, but they also face "over the limit" and "late payment penalties" which run the effective rate of interest up to more than 30 percent annually for many credit-card customers.

Writing for *CNNMoney.com* in April 2007, Gerri Willis described a number of ways the credit-card industry can rack up huge interest charges. "Universal default" allows an issuer to charge interest rates "as high as 35 percent." Late fees and other penalties result in "penalty interest rates" topping "30 percent in some cases."

Penalty fees once were capped by the law, but another U.S. Supreme Court ruling changed all of that. *Frontline* quotes Duncan MacDonald, then general counsel of Citibank's credit-card division, as later saying that the decision took the lid off late fees, which had been in the five- to ten-dollar range: "Fees quickly shot up from $15 to $29 to as high as $39. I certainly didn't imagine that someday we might've ended up creating Frankenstein."

There is so much money to be made from high interest rates, late payments, and other penalties that credit-card companies are playing the percentages and providing lines of credit to their customers far beyond what they could justify if the laws of usury were still in place. These loose lending standards set us up for the slow-moving train wreck that hit us with full force in the waning days of the Bush administration.

That "mountain load of DEBT" which Edward Everett warned us about back in the 1850's is with us again in the first decade of the 21st century. Something must be done about these credit excesses before the United States can regain her proper place as the foremost private-enterprise economy in the world.

The Coarsening of the Culture

"In the Name of God, Amen."
~The Mayflower Compact (1620)

"Men have forgotten God."
~Aleksandr Solzhenitsyn, "Templeton Lecture" (1983)

In his Templeton Lecture in London on May 10, 1983, the great Russian novelist Aleksandr Solzhenitsyn told a story from his childhood under communist rule: "More than half a century ago, while I was still a child, I recall hearing a number of older people offer the following explanation for the great disasters that had befallen Russia: 'Men have forgotten God; that's why all this has happened.'"

The Nobel laureate went on to describe how he spent 50 years studying the Russian Revolution only to come to the same conclusion:

> In the process I have read hundreds of books, collected hundreds of personal testimonies, and have already contributed eight volumes of my own toward the effort of clearing away the rubble left by that upheaval. But if I were asked today to formulate as concisely as possible the main cause of the ruinous Revolution that swallowed up some sixty million of our people, I could not put it more accurately than to repeat: "Men have forgotten God; that's why all this has happened."

Aleksandr Solzhenitsyn was a prophetic voice of opposition to communism whose insights into the inherent evil of the Soviet system were transformed into such moving works as *One Day in the Life of Ivan Denisovich*, *The Gulag Archipelago*, and *Cancer Ward*.

For his powerful critique of the communist regime, Solzhenitsyn was awarded the Nobel Prize for literature in 1970 and was invited to give the commencement address at Harvard University in 1978.

However, when he focused his critical eye on the West for succumbing to the temptations of materialism, the intelligentsia in Western Europe and the United States turned against him with a surprising ferocity, ignoring or denigrating his warning that we are, in our own way, susceptible to the "deadly virus" of a culture that has forgotten God.

As Solzhenitsyn clearly saw, the crisis of faith was not limited to those living under totalitarian regimes. Yes, those rulers attempted to use the power of the state to wipe out all vestiges of religious belief, but the disease they suffered from was "the principal trait of the entire twentieth century." "The failings of human consciousness, deprived of its divine dimension, have been a determining factor in all the major crimes of the century . . . the entire twentieth century is being sucked into the vortex of atheism and self-destruction."

Sent into exile to the West by the communists in 1974, the late Russian novelist still speaks to us today. Westerners may be free to practice their religion, he says, but Western Europe and the United States are losing their "religious consciousness." Western regimes risk collapsing from within, even in the absence of an external strategic threat.

Solzhenitsyn notes that "this gradual sapping of the strength from within is a threat to faith that is perhaps even more dangerous than any attempt to assault religion violently from without." More recently, Pope Benedict XVI has valiantly spoken out about the dangers of a "dictatorship of relativism" in Western Europe. The European Union has underscored its secular stance by making sure that its new constitution does not even mention the critical role of Christianity in building the great civilization of Western Europe.

It took a 19th-century Frenchman, Alexis de Tocqueville, to describe our American system and our way of life better than we could describe it ourselves in his remarkable work, *Democracy in America*. The most famous quotation attributed to Alexis de Tocqueville (and I confess that I have used it numerous times over the years) expresses a central truth about our society. "America is great because she is good," he said. "And, if she ever ceases to be good, she will cease to be great."

Scholars might question whether Tocqueville uttered those precise words, but they ring true, and so does his observation that "liberty cannot be established without morality, nor morality without faith." In this, Tocqueville recognized the strength of the American character, built on the observation of William Penn over a century earlier: "Those who will not be governed by the laws of God will be ruled by tyrants." By Tocqueville's time, the words of the founder of Pennsylvania had become ingrained in the American character, so that Tocqueville could report that "the Americans combine the notion of religion and liberty so intimately in their minds, that it is impossible to conceive of one without the other."

Solzhenitsyn's address, like his historical and literary works, is not a mere intellectual exercise. No, he is trying to warn us before it is too late that we have lost the combination of religious piety and liberty which once guided the fortunes of our nation.

In the wake of that loss, our nation's fortunes have changed — and so has our nation's character.

Can we still call ourselves a "good society" when nearly 50 million unborn babies have been aborted since the infamous 1973 Supreme Court decision *Roe* v. *Wade*, which wiped out all legal restraints on abortion in all fifty states?

Is America still a good society when our best-known export is the "culture" of Hollywood, which glamorizes sex, violence, crude language, and mindless hedonism?

Can we still claim to be a society guided by Christian morality when the mainstream media measures human worth in terms of a person's celebrity status or how many billions he has accumulated in business? What does it say about our culture when a "respected" private-equity chieftain brags that, in pursuing business deals, he wants to "inflict pain" and "kill off his rivals"?

Solzhenitsyn warns what happens to our children as the cultural elite of the Western world forgets God:

Western societies are losing more and more of their religious essence as they thoughtlessly yield up their younger generation to atheism. If a blasphemous film about Jesus is shown throughout the United States, reputedly one of the

103

most religious countries in the world, or a major newspaper publishes a shameless caricature of the Virgin Mary, what further evidence of godlessness does one need? When external rights are completely unrestricted, why should one make an inner effort to restrain oneself from ignoble acts?

Solzhenitsyn follows in the footsteps of another prophetic Russian novelist. Dostoyevsky, Solzhenitsyn points out, "drew from the French Revolution and its seething hatred of the Church the lesson that 'revolution must necessarily begin with atheism.'"

This loss of the religious underpinnings of our society has serious consequences, among them (Solzhenitsyn notes) a decline in our "civic courage." Think about it: We haven't had a president since Ronald Reagan (and, perhaps, Dwight Eisenhower before him) who has exemplified the characteristics of civic courage. Solzhenitsyn found this decline in civic courage "particularly noticeable among the ruling and intellectual elites."

T.R. Fehrenbach, the great Texas historian, once compared our current crop of national political leaders to our Founding Fathers:

> We should wallow in political talent compared with colonial times. Certainly we should grow more than the tiny states that produced George Washington, John Adams, James Madison, Benjamin Franklin, James Monroe, Alexander Hamilton, John Jay and Thomas Jefferson. No way. The democratic process has boiled down to a choice between two disappointments. Is it not odd that the most productive and powerful nation on Earth seemingly cannot reproduce the intellectual and moral political giants of its first generations?

The majority of Americans, I believe, sense this absence of civic courage among our leaders but do not know what to do about it. Since our choices seem so limited, Americans become increasingly disengaged from our political system unless a particular issue (such as George W. Bush's immigration-reform legislation in 2007) comes along and so upsets them that they make their anger known to those in power. But such eruptions are usually temporary.

In his Harvard commencement address, Solzhenitsyn laid out the essence of conservatism when he reminded his audience that the original motto of Harvard University was *"Veritas"* — "truth," in the Latin that every Harvard student was once required to master in his undergraduate years. Solzhenitsyn discovered that truth in the Soviet gulag. Not everyone who was sent to the brutal prison camps had the same experience; but for Solzhenitsyn, it was profound. Amidst the deprivation and stark surroundings, he learned to focus on what is truly important in life.

Sadly, Solzhenitsyn's powerful critique of our culture has been studiously ignored by most of those in a position to address the concerns he raised in 1978 at Harvard and in 1983 in his Templeton Address. Our nation's intellectual elite undoubtedly recognized that Solzhenitsyn represented a mortal threat to their reign. They made him virtually an invisible man, even as Americans searched for the means to reverse the decline of our culture.

Remarkably few of those who have emerged as the self-proclaimed spokesmen for conservatism in the post-Reagan era of American politics ever mention Solzhenitsyn in making the case for conservative principles. Notable exceptions include the publication of the *Solzhenitsyn Reader* by the Intercollegiate Studies Institute (ISI) in 2006, and an appreciation of Solzhenitsyn's wisdom in the pages of *Chronicles: A Magazine of American Culture*. Joseph Pearce wrote in the August 2007 issue of *Chronicles* that Solzhenitsyn's "indispensable Harvard address . . . still serves as a touchstone or litmus test of true conservatism." How right Pearce is.

Solzhenitsyn's diagnosis of our ills and his suggestions as to how to reclaim our culture are like a road map back to the "good society" we inherited. Should we ignore him and continue to drift blindly, the words of a race car enthusiast come to mind: "The only way you can coast is downhill."

Solzhenitsyn presents six themes that are deserving of our careful consideration. First, as he declared in his Templeton Address, the tide of secularism is sapping our strength from within: "This gradual sapping of strength from within is a threat to faith that is perhaps even more dangerous than any attempt to assault religion violently from without."

The American people are well ahead of their political leaders in sensing that our moral compass has gone dreadfully wrong. A May 2007 Gallup Poll reports that 82 percent of Americans believe that the state of moral values in the country as a whole is growing worse. Seventy-four percent said that their overall perception of our moral values is negative.

The Economist, noting that the award-winning HBO series *The Sopranos* has become a leading U.S. export, declared that "American culture . . . revels in overturning moral certitudes."

> American culture has always had a weakness for sex and violence. But since the 1960s it has gleefully eliminated conventional distinctions between good and bad, and since the 1990s it has been supercharged by the dramatic increase in the power of mass communications that are bringing America's cultural offerings to every corner of the world. The success of "The Sopranos," both commercially and critically, can only serve to reinforce this trend. The tensions created by the growing global reach of shows like "The Sopranos," may prove far more difficult to manage in the long run than the tensions created by the passing neoconservative moment.

Even the self-professed atheist and pro-abortion "libertarian Democrat" Camille Paglia can see the deleterious effects on the arts of our increasingly secularized culture: "A totally secularized society with contempt for religion sinks into materialism and self-absorption and gradually goes slack, without leaving an artistic legacy . . . For the fine arts to revive, they must recover their spiritual center."

Joseph Cardinal Ratzinger, later elected Pope Benedict XVI, has been equally blunt in decrying the tide of secularism rising throughout the Western world. This "dictatorship of relativism," he argues, threatens to lead us into a new "Dark Age." Even some prominent nonbelievers in Europe have come to take seriously Pope Benedict's words about the collapse of the continent's moral foundations. The late Oriana Fallaci, an Italian social commentator who was a fierce critic of the rising tide of Islam, coined the term *Eurabia* to describe the future of Europe if Europeans did not come to their senses. Before she died, Fallaci proclaimed that "only the writings of Ratzinger" gave her hope for the future of Western civilization.

Catholic sociologist Franco Garelli argues that the pressing need in Europe is "to reactivate . . . the values of the Christian faith and ethical guideposts derived from it," which is what Pope Benedict seems determined to do.

Europe faces profound identity problems, but America is deeply mired in a "dictatorship of relativism" of her own. We call it "diversity"—and it represents a death wish for civilized life. "Diversity" has become a central weapon in the lexicon of ACLU-types who want to rid America of any vestige of Christian morality. It is often used to challenge the right of communities to establish their own standards, in their schools and in their neighborhoods. In public schools, the left-leaning teachers' unions push their pro-abortion, pro-homosexuality agendas into the curriculum, while rooting out any remnant of common-sense morality that might preserve their students from the rampant plague of sexually transmitted diseases. The fact that public schools spend more and more to teach students less and less does not seem to faze them

The same mentality threatens communities across the country, as pro-pornography lawyers from New York or Los Angeles swoop down to defend sexually oriented businesses and to challenge common-sense ordinances that prohibit or regulate them. In the name of "free speech" and "free expression," these purveyors of libertinism insist that "everything is permitted"—everything, that is, except the simple, basic moral truths of the Christian tradition. Unfettered by moral standards, this celebration of self-indulgence destroys any sense of civic virtue or moral duty. It introduces a social free-for-all, in which normal people are now demanded to accept things that were once universally recognized as moral travesties. These advocates of "divine decadence" even want us to congratulate them for their "bravery" in advocating this rupture of our moral tradition. They do not want our society simply to coast downhill; they want to push it there.

It is not simple to combat the powerful forces of cultural hedonism. Attacks on the Christian faith, popular in the West ever since the "Death of God" craze of some 40 years ago, appear even stronger today. Best-selling books by the likes of journalist Christopher Hitchens, British professor Richard Dawkins, and French philosopher Michel Onfray denounce Christianity. Hitchens' title states his thesis: *god is not Great: How Religion Poisons Everything* (the lack of capital letters on the first three words is intentional). Hitchens is apparently convinced, in the words of *The Economist*, that "the world would be better off without religion altogether. Stupid religious people would stop fighting stupid religious wars and a new enlightenment would ensue." Hitchens, who earlier won acclaim in antireligious circles for his vicious attack on the late Mother Teresa in the pages of *Vanity Fair*, seems to ignore much about those regimes that bear primary responsibility for the major wars of the 20th century—the pagan Nazi regime of Adolf Hitler and atheistic communist regimes in Russia, China, North Korea, and North Vietnam. And he conveniently drops down the memory hole the granddaddy of them all: the French Revolution, with its "enlightened" barbarism.

Richard Dawkins, an apostle of Darwin, is the author of *The God Delusion*, which proclaims that "atheists are generally smarter than Christians." To which Joe Sobran replied, "I wouldn't doubt it. After all, St. Paul says God has chosen the foolish people of this world to confound the wise."

Michel Onfray's *Atheist Manifesto: The Case Against Christianity, Judaism, and Islamism* has sold 300,000 copies in France. Reviewing the book in the *Financial Times*, historian Paul Johnson remarked: "Onfray sticks to the view that the French Enlightenment and Revolution were the pivotal events of history to which all things led and from which all has followed." The great Russian novelist Fyodor Dostoyevsky would not disagree with Professor Onfray, although he saw the chain of events in a vastly different light: "Revolution must necessarily begin with atheism," wrote Dostoyevsky. The great question facing humanity is "Does God exist?" As Ivan Karamazov says, "If there is no God, everything is permitted." Orthodox Archbishop Hilarion Alfeyev, the representative of the Russian Orthodox Church to the European Institutions in Brussels, points out that "If there is no God, there is no absolute scale of moral values, and all the values are relative. I think that Dostoyesky's power is in that he showed in all his works that salvation and morality are impossible without God."

Now that the left has banished God from American public life, Ivan Karamazov's vision is becoming reality. Fifty years ago, even Planned Parenthood understood that abortion was murder. Yet it now rakes in millions performing more abortions than any other "provider" in the country. And think about that word, *provider*: What does it "provide"? Death to innocent human beings.

Our grandparents all understood that homosexuality was wrong— but now Barney Frank wants to make sure that "gays and lesbians and transgenders" have the same rights as "minorities" against job discrimination that blacks do. And public schools, which were founded in the 19th century to provide a common sense of civic virtue grounded in daily prayer, rigorous learning, and moral living, no longer allow prayer or even the affirmation of God's existence.

According to British author John Gray, "secular fundamentalism" (which seeks to cordon off religion from public life) is a dead end. Gray makes the case that "the secular era is in the past." If he is right, then the anti-Christian polemics of Hitchens, Dawkins, and Onfray may be a dying gasp—signals that the tide of secularism may be retreating.

While everything else is permitted in our current secular age, God is not. Every age has had its sophists who promise wealth and power to their acolytes. These movements and their errors come and go like the tide, but conservatives believe in the permanent things. "The essence of social conservatism," Russell Kirk wrote, "is preservation of the ancient moral traditions of humanity." The gods of diversity and modernity defy those traditions, but they are not alone. The gods of materialism are also legion.

The second theme of Solzhenitsyn's work that continues to speak to us is the failure to value material possessions properly. As Solzhenitsyn puts it:

> The endless accumulation of possessions? That will not bring fulfillment either. (Discerning individuals have long since understood that possessions must be subordinated to other, higher principles, that they must have a spiritual

justification, a mission; otherwise, as Nikolai Berdyaev put it, they bring ruin to human life, becoming the tools of avarice and oppression.)

Earlier, I mentioned Stephen Schwarzman, the private-equity mogul who is the principal at Blackstone. The *Wall Street Journal* calls Schwarzman, a classmate and friend of President George W. Bush when the two were at Yale, the "$7 billion Man." The Wall Street financier gave a very revealing interview to the *Journal* on June 13, 2007, only weeks before Blackstone's IPO.

A consummate deal maker, Schwarzman "views each deal as a contest to the death," according to the *Journal*. "I want war—not a series of skirmishes. I always think about what will kill off the other bidder." Solzhenitsyn described businessmen like Stephen Schwarzman well: "Cold calculation holds sway in business relations, and has even become accepted as normal behavior. To yield in some way to an opponent or competitor is considered an unforgivable blunder for the party having an advantage in position, power, or wealth." (Aristotle described him well, too. Materialistic men have no use for leisure or for the development of their higher moral powers. Hence they are natural slaves.) The *Journal*'s probing produced some gems. When Schwarzman was asked by a family member if he needed "any more money," his own mother interrupted and answered: "You don't understand what drives him. Money is the measuring stick."

Stephen Schwarzman is a perfect example of what the new "Masters of the Universe" do with their unprecedented wealth:

> Mr. Schwarzman is exacting in his personal life too. Once, while sunning by the pool at his 11,000-square-foot home in Palm Beach, Fla., he complained to Jean-Pierre Zeugin, his executive chef and estate manager, that an employee wasn't wearing the proper black shoes with his uniform, according to Mr. Zeugin, who says he has great admiration for his boss. Mr. Schwarzman explains that he found the squeak of the rubber soles distracting. He expects lunches consisting of cold soup, a cold entrée such as lobster salad or fresh

grilled tuna on salad, followed by dessert, Mr. Zeugin says. He eats the three-course meal within 15 minutes, the chef says. Mr. Zeugin says he often spends $3,000 for a weekend of food for Mr. Schwarzman and his wife, including stone crabs that cost $400, or $40 per claw.

John Wilder, another finance engineer, took over as president and CEO of Texas Utilities, one of the most-respected companies in my state, in 2004. The Dallas-based utility company had been led to prominence by such outstanding Texans as the late Louis Austin, who had the foresight to build a nuclear plant in the 1970's to address our state's looming energy needs. TXU, as it later became known, got into financial trouble a number of years ago through some bad investment decisions made by Austin's successor as CEO. Wilder, an outsider known for his financial acumen, was brought in to run the company and immediately started performing his "financial magic." Three years later, Wilder cashed out for more than $250 million, after selling TXU to a private equity group which loaded the company up with billions of dollars in debt. Not bad for three years of work at a publicly regulated utility.

What has happened to American business since the 1960's? Back then, Barry Goldwater enlisted supporters of "free enterprise" to fight the liberal push toward socialism. At the time, with tax rates as high as 90 percent and some leftist magazine editorials virtually indistinguishable from Communist Party propaganda, socialism was a real threat. In the decades that followed, the generation of business leaders that emerged in the friendlier economic atmosphere seemed to take the moral issues for granted. (So, for that matter, did Barry Goldwater in 1960: his *Conscience of a Conservative* addressed economic and national-security issues, but education was the only "family" issue he discussed.) The result is that ethical values in the business community have gone into decline, along with the rest of our culture. My friends used to kid me that "military intelligence" (the branch in which I served in the U.S. Army) was an oxymoron. But "business ethics" is no joke these days. Must we choose between unbridled capitalism and creeping socialism? Can't we do better?

Peggy Noonan described this new "Gilded Age" in a *Wall Street Journal* piece in July 2007:

> The gap between rich and poor is great, and there is plenty
> of want, and also confusion. What the superrich do for a
> living now often seems utterly incomprehensible, and has
> for at least a generation. There is no word for it, only an im-
> age. There's a big pile of coins on a table. The rich shove
> their hands in, raise them, and as the coins sift through
> their fingers it makes . . . a bigger pile of coins. Then they
> sift through it again and the pile gets bigger again.

Noonan sees the tendency to measure human worth in terms
of possessions as another step in the coarsening of our culture:

> There are good things and bad in the Gilded Age, pluses
> and minuses. I write here of a minus. It has to do with our
> manners, the ones we show each other on the street. I think
> riches, or the pursuit of riches, has made us ruder. You'd
> think broad comfort would assuage certain hungers. It has
> not. It has sharpened them.

Noonan could have pointed to Aristotle. In his *Nicomachean
Ethics*, the philosopher spelled out the central importance of civic
virtue, which includes goodwill to others, even strangers. The
self-indulgent killer instinct can thrive alongside the celebration
of "diversity," but only in a society that has more in common with
Thomas Hobbes' state of nature than in what we once knew as
America the Beautiful.

Tom Wolfe describes the "new rich" who inhabit Greenwich,
Connecticut, and run many of our leading hedge funds. Borrowing
a theme from his novel *The Bonfire of the Vanities*, he finds today's
new "masters of the universe" "even coarser and ruder than their
predecessors could have ever imagined being":

> What is it that makes these people so angry and nasty? . . .
> most of these people are in their late thirties and early to

mid forties. For men making, in many cases, tens of millions and up per year, they qualify as young. They talk about business in young-warrior metaphors: "pulling the trigger" (making huge risky bets on the market); "mowing them all down" (overpowering companies that try to block your strategies); "This is war!" (get out of my way—or else I'll make you suffer); "Surrender your booty!" (I'm a corporate raider poised to take over your company); "We don't eat what we don't kill" (if you, the investor, don't make a profit, then we in the hedge fund's management don't take a profit ourselves, something oddly true in spirit—although ... not in fact). These people tend to be bright and well-educated, many at Harvard, Princeton, and other top-ranked colleges. They come from well-educated families. They still enjoy the virgin animal health of youth. They are flush with optimism and confidence, as well as money. With all that going for them, what inna nameagod is their problem?

Their problem has been underscored in every generation for a hundred years. In 1939 Mortimer Adler observed that even the best colleges had not offered a decent education since the turn of the century. In 1947, Dorothy Sayers bemoaned the death of logic in conversation. In 1959, William F. Buckley, Jr., agreed. By the time Allan Bloom wrote *The Closing of the American Mind* in 1987, he was in a minority when he observed that most of his students were relativists. That generation of students has grown up to be today's Masters of the Universe. They thrive on diversity's destruction of community. If there is no common truth, we have nothing in common, and no duties to one another. Unlike "Cool Hand Luke," there is no "failure to communicate"; there's simply nothing to communicate. Pull the trigger.

The third theme in Solzhenitsyn's work that continues to ring true today is that the decline of our culture is reflected in the quality of our art and literature:

For several decades now, world literature, music, painting, and sculpture have exhibited a stubborn tendency to grow

not higher, but to the side, not toward the highest achievements of craftsmanship and of the human spirit, but toward
their disintegration into a frantic and insidious "novelty." To
decorate public spaces we put up sculptures that aestheti-
cize pure ugliness—but we no longer register surprise. And
if visitors from outer space were to pick up our music over
the airwaves, how could they ever guess that earthlings once
had a Bach, a Beethoven, and a Schubert, now abandoned
as out of date and obsolete?

The disease detected by Solzhenitsyn affects the entire human
experience. He sees the profound decline of our culture reflected
everywhere.

Since Plato, mankind has understood that the arts are the salient and central ingredient of civilization. What shocks Solzhenitsyn
is the apparent lack of concern of our moral and cultural leaders
as the aesthetic pillars of our communities collapse. An article
by Peter Plagens in *Newsweek* in 2007 asked, "Which is the Most
Influential Work of Art of the Last 100 Years?" Plagens offered five
choices: a urinal ("Fountain"), by Marcel Duchamp; "Black Square,"
by Kazimir Malevich; "Campbell's Soup Can," by Andy Warhol;
an abstract by Jackson Pollock titled "One (Number 31)"; and
Pablo Picasso's "Les Demoiselles d'Avignon," which "depicts nude
women in a brothel."

And the winner is "Les Demoiselles D'Avignon," which even
the *Newsweek* writer is forced to acknowledge is "still pretty ugly.
Well, maybe not ugly-ugly, but certainly hard to take."

Plagens quotes Matisse, who said of the painting when he first
saw it, "how raw, cacophonic and nasty it looked." What does it say
about the state of our culture when such a painting is regarded as
"the most influential work of art in the last 100 years"?

The next 100 years are not looking much better. The rage in
2007 was a bizarre piece entitled "For the Love of God" by Damien
Hirst. As described by the *Financial Times*,

"For the Love of God" is a life-size cast of a human skull
in platinum that is covered entirely by 8,601 pavé-set dia-

monds. The Hirst "creation" has a price tag of $100 million, and the diamonds are said to be worth more than $20 million. The celebration of death corresponds fully to the destruction of all life in contemporary art—except, of course, for a life wallowing in squalor. In an interview with the Times, Hirst even appears to praise great wealth as "the ultimate victory over death, the most you could get from decoration because our society loves money and wealth."

Peter Aspden of the *Financial Times* describes one of Hirst's "religious works":

> In "The Adoration", Hirst reconstructs the nativity scene in his own way: three sheep kneel in supplication to a sterling-silver baby, housed in an incubation unit. Hirst describes it as a "retelling" of the nativity story "but with three dead sheep praying to a silver foetus". Considering this moment celebrates the birth of Christ, there is not much sense of life there, I say. "There is the life of the art," he replies quick as a flash.

As the article notes, "disillusionment with religion is a recurring theme" in Hirst's works. It surely has not hurt him at the cash register. Hirst's "art" has garnered him a personal fortune of $260 million. He is "hotter and richer than ever," according to the *Sunday Times* Rich List.

The triumph of avant-garde modernism in art during the 20th century would take volumes to explain, but Camille Paglia has observed one common element: "With few exceptions, most modern artists and intellectuals were agnostics or atheists, above all in Europe, where anti-clericalism has raged since the Enlightenment." Neither Picasso nor Hirst is an exception to that rule.

Paglia is not impressed with what the modernists have wrought. "The state of the humanities in the U.S. can be measured by present achievement: would anyone seriously argue that the fine arts or even popular culture is enjoying a period of high originality and creativity?" she asks. Her prescription will make the elites gag on their stone crabs: "I would argue that the route to a renaissance of the American fine arts lies through religion."

The fourth insight that we can glean from Solzhenitsyn's work is that a system based on the letter of the law has replaced laws based on an ethical foundation:

> People in the West have acquired considerable skill in us-
> ing, interpreting, and manipulating law (though laws tend
> to be too complicated for an average person to understand
> without the help of an expert). Every conflict is solved ac-
> cording to the letter of the law and this is considered to be
> the ultimate solution. If one is right from a legal point of
> view, nothing more is required, nobody may mention that
> one could still not be entirely right, and urge self-restraint
> or a renunciation of these rights, call for sacrifice and self-
> less risk: This would simply sound absurd . . . I have spent
> all my life under a Communist regime and I will tell you
> that a society without any objective legal scale is a terrible
> one indeed. But a society with no other scale but the legal
> one is also less than worthy of man. A society based on
> the letter of the law and never reaching any higher fails to
> take advantage of the full range of human possibilities. The
> letter of the law is too cold and formal to have a beneficial
> influence on society. Whenever the tissue of life is woven of
> legalistic relationships, this creates an atmosphere of spiri-
> tual mediocrity that paralyzes man's noblest impulses.

When men forget God, they abandon traditional moral codes, too. And so our system of laws, once expressly based on the natural-law tradition and English common law, has given way to a system based on the letter of the law at the very moment when "diversity" excuses us from having to agree on anything in common, including what the letter of the law really means. Like Tocqueville, Solzhenitsyn understands the problem more than our leaders do.

In a society trapped in the tyranny of relativism, the letter of the law cannot refer back to anything we have in common—any truth, any tradition, even any common opinion. There is no community that can sustain such common truths. Instead, the letter of the law refers back only to itself, and, in the wonderful phrase that Faust identifies with the Devil, "blooms every day anew."

Federalist 62 warns of the dangers of an overly legalistic society:

> It will be of little avail to the people that the laws are made
> by men of their own choice, if the laws be so voluminous
> that they cannot be read, or so incoherent that they cannot
> be understood; if they be repealed or revised before they are
> promulgated, or undergo such incessant changes that no
> man who knows what the law is today can guess what it will
> be tomorrow. Law is defined to be a rule of action; but how
> can that be a rule, which is little known and less fixed?

An excessively legalistic system leads to a society in which lobbyists exercise far greater influence over the legislative process than average citizens as they seek to shape laws to the advantage of their clients—and to the disadvantage of nearly everyone else. The greater the number of laws and the bigger government is at every level, the greater the need to hire lobbyists to protect one's interests. Our congressmen in Washington and the legislators in the various states have become more attuned to the wishes and concerns of the lobby than to those of their own constituents, who cannot keep up with an ever-changing and increasingly complicated array of laws.

Add to this mix the pressure that can be applied by mainstream media outlets to pass legislation they are interested in. Wanting to curry favor with the media, legislators are often all too willing to back those bills that they believe will help advance their political careers—whatever the impact on the common good.

Meanwhile, middle-class citizens, who do not have lobbyists in Washington, D.C., or in the state capitals, are increasingly forgotten, and their interests neglected or ignored to the detriment of society.

When the law and judicial decisions are viewed only through the prism of "individual rights," ignoring any sense of "human obligations," the common good is undermined. The individual's rights cannot be separated from his responsibilities—and for most of history, those responsibilities have come first. But federal-court decisions in recent decades have been particularly absolutist and legalistic in pushing individual rights so far that any mention of "responsibilities" is considered at best an anachronism and at worst unconstitutional. Thus the guarantee of "free speech" in the Bill of Rights becomes an "absolute right" allowing profiteers to exploit our base instincts by flooding film, TV, and periodicals with all manner of pornography, obscenity, vulgarity, and violence.

Solzhenitsyn describes the dangers to a society in which such freedom turns into license, where

> destructive and irresponsible freedom has been granted
> boundless space. Society has turned out to have scarce
> defense against the abyss of human decadence, for example
> against the misuse of liberty for moral violence against
> young people, such as motion pictures full of pornography,
> crime, and horror. This is all considered to be part of free-
> dom and to be counterbalanced, in theory, by the young
> people's right not to look and not to accept. Life organized
> legalistically has thus shown its inability to defend itself
> against the corrosion of evil.

Can anyone seriously argue that the moral sewer created by our Hollywood culture and our pornography industry has not led to a serious coarsening of our culture? We once had standards in our movie industry, a code of conduct that the studios followed and which acted as a restraint against "the misuse of liberty for moral violence against young people." But that code was abandoned decades ago. Moreover, federal-court decisions, based on the notion of "absolute free speech," have made it virtually impossible for communities to rein in this exploitation of sex and violence for material gain.

Many federal judges have taken their "letter of the law" decision-making to the extreme by interpreting the Freedom of Religion Clause of the First Amendment to erect a "wall of separation" between religion and the public square. In practice, that means the total removal of any mention of God as a guiding force in public life. Even liberal Supreme Court Justice William O. Douglas once affirmed that "We are a religious people whose institutions presuppose the existence of a Supreme Being." But legal extremists have taken aim at the religious foundations of our institutions. Public schools not only deny Christian morality as a standard by which our conduct should be measured; they remove any mention of the Christian tradition as the source of our freedoms. Today's crusaders against religion treat earlier generations of Americans—who believed in God and prayed to Him in our schools—as benighted, backward, and bigoted.

Unelected federal judges have used their power to foist their own political opinions on entire communities and states, all in the name of individual rights. They abolished any laws limiting abortion in all 50 states after discovering a constitutional "right" of privacy. They destroyed neighborhood schools through the forced busing of schoolchildren. They overturned local electoral systems on the flimsiest claims of protecting minority rights. They mandated "racial balancing" through the construction of public housing projects in select neighborhoods, despite the opposition of homeowners. And they seized control of state and local prison systems from the legislative branch of government and put their overseers in charge of our criminal-justice system.

This emphasis on rights rather than responsibilities is a reflection of the egalitarianism that fueled the French Revolution rather than the principles of the American Revolution. It has led inexorably to a labyrinth of laws and regulations based on "gender" and race, ostensibly to "level the playing field." But the laws are often carried to the extreme, requiring universities to provide equal funding for female athletic teams, even though public interest in male sports teams is far greater. At universities throughout the country, traditional men's sports such as wrestling, lacrosse, and crew have been abolished, while lavish scholarship programs have been developed for women who can play field hockey.

I know from personal experience the disruption that can be caused by this emphasis on rights over duties. Many years ago, an Anglo woman from Richardson, Texas, worked as the receptionist of a small oil-and-gas company in Austin that was a subsidiary of the venture-capital firm for which I worked. She had married a Muslim from the Middle East, converted to Islam, and decided that she had to wear her *hijab* to work. The president of the company was already unhappy with her job performance. When she refused his request not to wear her Muslim headdress at the office, he terminated her. She then filed a "religious discrimination" complaint with the federal Equal Employment Opportunity Commission, and later sued the company. Even though her deposition revealed that she was selective in her adherence to Islamic beliefs, the company was forced to settle the case because of concerns about litigation exposure. It was a classic example of the unintended consequences of an overly legalistic system that emphasizes rights to the exclusions of duties or obligations.

The fifth thing we can still learn from Solzhenitsyn is how completely the concept of good and evil has been replaced by political correctness:

> The concepts of good and evil have been ridiculed for several centuries; banished from common use, they have been replaced by political or class considerations of short-lived value. It has become embarrassing to appeal to eternal concepts, embarrassing to state that evil makes its home in the individual human heart before it enters a political system. Yet it is not considered shameful to make daily concessions to an integral evil. Judging by the continuing landslide of concessions made before the eyes of our own generation alone, the West is ineluctably slipping toward the abyss.

I have often marveled at how virtually every cause and faction that has arisen under the banner of "diversity" has been anything but "diverse." They have taken aim at everything in the social and political order that supports an ordered society guided by moral principles. In practice, "diversity" is permitted only when the cause in question is opposed to our traditions and the institutions that have made us a free people. In practice, "diversity" always seems to mean affirmative action for homosexuals, rather than the freedom of Christian employees to gather in prayer in the lunchroom. It always seems to mean bringing in high-budget consultants to offer workshops on how not to offend homosexuals rather than how best to harmonize a heterosexual marriage with the demands of one's job. As former senator Howard Baker would say, as far as the "diversity" tyrants go, that door doesn't swing both ways.

The Founding Fathers recognized that there would always be enemies of freedom. In fact, they understood that the greatest threat to freedom was not any foreign enemy but political leaders' lust for power. In order to acquire such power and to keep it, the ideologue will deform language to suit his ends. That is why Confucius said that the first step in restoring order in a degenerate society is to restore the proper meaning of words. In the West, from Aristotle on, it has been understood that liberty cannot long survive the perversion of language.

Lenin said that one of the most important tools of ideology was the dictionary, and Stalin wrote a famous piece on the critical use of vocabulary in ideology. Like Karl Marx, who declared war on traditional philosophy in 1841, the modern left uses ideology and education as vital weapons in their effort to destroy tradition and freedom.

So we should not be surprised that the egalitarianism that gave us the Terror of the French Revolution should today be disguised as "diversity." Businesses, government agencies, classrooms at every level, the military, and our entire culture are saturated with the worship of "diversity." That is why Pope Benedict's words offer so much insight: There is no "diversity from diversity," there is only conformity or ostracism and, in virtually every setting, punishment.

The notion of egalitarianism does not exist in a vacuum. It has long been a very successful staple of ideological programs committed to the destruction of liberty. Of course, equality is never an end in itself. From Hobbes to Rousseau to Mao, it has merely been a tool, the dagger that cuts the heart out of liberty and makes absolute power possible. The tyrant steps in, resuscitates the cadaver, imposes his tyranny, and produces a Frankenstein's monster. As early as Socrates, the West has recognized that the rule of the tyrant is a war against human nature, social order, "the laws of nature and of nature's God," and ultimately, reality itself.

The final lesson that Solzhenitsyn continues to offer us today concerns the lack of Christian unity:

> In recent years the major Christian churches have taken steps toward reconciliation. But these measures are far too slow; the world is perishing a hundred times more quickly. No one expects the churches to merge or to revise all their doctrines, but only to present a common front against atheism. Yet even for such a purpose the steps taken are much too slow.

Solzhenitsyn argues that Christian unity is necessary in order "to present a common front against atheism." Yet it is not just atheism that is a threat to our civilization. A weakened and divided Christianity is ill prepared to withstand the forces of radical Islam, determined to extend Islamic dominance over every nation.

Divisions among Christians make it more difficult for us to preserve the essential character of Western civilization, inspired by the truths of natural law. Christians are not only divided among Catholics, Protestants, and Orthodox; we are divided within our congregations as well. As a Catholic, I saw in my lifetime a move to create an American Catholic Church that would have allowed individual Catholics to "pick and choose" the doctrines to which they would adhere. This "cafeteria Catholicism" was very pronounced in the United States, Western Europe, and Latin America during the late 1960's and throughout the 1970's. In countries such as Nicaragua, Brazil, and Peru, for example, "liberation theology" and "Christian Marxism" became the rage. This momentum for "independent" Catholic churches has waned in recent decades as Pope John Paul II and Pope Benedict XVI have emphasized universal adherence to the fundamental teachings of the Catholic Church.

Mainstream Protestantism in the United States has faced similar internal splits. Methodists, Episcopalians, Presbyterians, and Lutherans have all had bitter internecine battles for control between the traditionalists in their denominations and those who want to adapt their beliefs to the values of our modern secular society.

Those demanding change in the doctrines of mainstream Protestantism have generally prevailed within the United States and England, thus driving many of their members into the arms of "Bible-based" churches that have been more resistant to secularization. Until recently, the Southern Baptists had been a major beneficiary of increased numbers of people leaving mainstream Protestant denominations. Yet the Southern Baptists have their own divisions, as anyone who lives in Texas knows well. There have been lengthy battles over control of the Southern Baptist Convention and the Texas General Assembly by various factions within that denomination.

Consider the Roman Catholic Church and the Eastern Orthodox Churches, which split in the 11th century and have been feuding ever since—even though they share many beliefs on matters of faith and morals. Moreover, the Orthodox faithful are divided themselves, with their independent national churches having various doctrinal and disciplinary differences of their own.

It seems that Christian denominations spend more time in internal disputes or fighting one another than in working together first to halt and then reverse the cultural decline of our society. Until Christians put aside their differences and adopt a united front against what Pope Benedict XVI calls the "dictatorship of relativism," the coarsening of our culture will continue unabated.

Lest we forget, Christian disunity once paved the way for the aggressive expansion of Islam. Will such disunity lead to similar results today?

FINDING OUR WAY BACK

An Overview

"I don't want the cheese. I just want out of the trap."

~Bill Bowen

It is a lot easier to get into a big mess than it is to get out of it. To be blunt, our country is in one big mess. And most Americans realize it: A Gallup Poll taken in late 2008 revealed that 87 percent of the American people are dissatisfied with the way things are in the United States and think we are headed in the wrong direction.

We Americans are a funny lot. Sometimes it takes a full-blown crisis to wake us up to the seriousness of our problems. Well, we ought to be awake now. The credit crunch, excessive government spending, unsustainable trade and budget deficits, a foreign policy that is not effective in addressing the threat of radical Islam, and the continuing coarsening of our culture are a lethal combination. Unless we act quickly to reverse these negative trends, our children and our grandchildren are going to pay a heavy price for the mistakes of our leadership class.

Barack Obama capitalized on this wave of public discontent to win the presidency. "Change" may have been a great slogan to campaign on, but "change" is not a plan. It is no substitute for a carefully thought out strategy to address the serious problems we face. Barack Obama was very effective in sensing the mood of the voters and telling them what he thought they wanted to hear. But all too often it seemed as though he was talking out of both sides of his mouth—for example, telling the cultural left that he was in fundamental agreement with them on such issues as unlimited abortion rights, legalization of same-sex unions, and gun control, while downplaying those positions when speaking in socially conservative areas. On economic policy, he told some groups he strongly supported free trade while telling others, especially in industrial states, that he was concerned with the loss of manufacturing jobs and would look out for their interests. Yet his major appointees to oversee economic policy in his administration have been protégés of Wall Street investment banker and former Clinton Treasury Secretary Robert Rubin, an advocate of globalization and a strong supporter (as well as a beneficiary) of the Bush administration's bailout of such troubled Wall Street financial institutions as Citibank, where Rubin worked until early 2008. Moreover, Obama selected Ron Kirk to be his trade representative. Kirk, a former mayor of Dallas, is a strong advocate of free trade and a longtime lobbyist for major business interests.

When it comes to foreign policy, Barack Obama campaigned against the war in Iraq; yet he appointed as his White House chief of staff Rahm Emanuel, who, as a Democratic member of Congress, was a strong supporter of the war. Emanuel belongs to the neoliberal wing of the Democratic Party, which pushed for U.S. military intervention against the Serbs in Kosovo as well as a preemptive war in Iraq.

The more things change in Washington, the more they remain the same.

The new President did make some good appointments in his early selections—for instance, retired Gen. Jim Jones as director of the National Security Council (NSC) and Robert Gates, whom Obama kept on as secretary of defense. Yet how much influence will General Jones and Secretary Gates have with Hillary Clinton as secretary of state and Rahm Emanuel as chief of staff?

And the real question remains: Does President Obama have a strategic plan to get things back on the right track, or is he simply another Jimmy Carter—good at telling Americans how bad things are, but woefully inadequate when it comes to fixing what is wrong?

You cannot solve serious problems without an effective plan and the right people to implement it. I learned that lesson a long time ago when I was a young Army intelligence officer stationed along the Cambodian border in Vietnam. No matter how many soldiers we sent off to fight in that war, no matter how much money LBJ and Richard Nixon spent on waging it, our political and military strategy was fundamentally flawed from its beginning in the early days of the Kennedy administration. That policy was formulated by Secretary of Defense Robert Strange McNamara and his civilian "whiz kids" at the Pentagon who, in spite of their lofty IQs and elite pedigrees, knew far too much that was not true. (The neoconservative civilian crowd on Vice President Cheney's staff and at the Department of Defense, who orchestrated our preemptive war in Iraq, were eerily reminiscent of the McNamara crowd in their lack of understanding of the unintended consequences that their policies would unleash.)

The Robert McNamara—McGeorge Bundy elites, along with some of our military leaders in Vietnam (Gen. Creighton Abrams being a notable exception), never understood the nature of the enemy we were fighting. This was particularly telling since the leading communist strategist in North Vietnam, Truong Chinh, laid out in his works *The Protracted War* and *The Revolution Will Win* the strategy the communists would follow to defeat first the French and then the Americans.

The fall of Saigon in 1975 would not have happened had we developed and implemented an effective strategy when we first sent a small contingent of American troops to South Vietnam in support of President Ngo Dinh Diem in the early days of the Kennedy administration. Contrast our failed strategy in Vietnam with President Reagan's successful strategy to win the Cold War and defeat the Soviet Union with very little loss of American lives. Who would have thought that possible in the late 1970's, given the fall of Saigon, the Soviet invasion of Afghanistan, the seizure of American hostages by the radical regime in Iran, and the post-Vietnam "malaise" of the Carter administration?

Reagan not only put a comprehensive strategy in place but chose the right men to execute it (Bill Clark at NSC, Bill Casey at the CIA, and Cap Weinberger at the Department of Defense). It worked: The Soviet Empire is no more.

Militant Islam is an even greater threat to Western civilization than international communism was. Radical Muslims seek to impose their views and way of life on the entire world and are willing to die on behalf of their cause. Their strong yet misguided faith can only be effectively challenged by a committed core of Christian believers (and their allies). That was the case when Christian forces routed a much larger Turkish naval force at the Battle of Lepanto in 1571. To diminish the influence of radical Islam, we must start by putting the right strategy and effective leaders in place.

We also need an economic policy designed to put America back to work by encouraging job creation in the private sector. In the late 1970's, we had high taxes, double-digit inflation, and high unemployment ("stagflation"). President Reagan set forth—and got a Democratic-controlled Congress to approve—an economic policy that cut taxes across the board, reduced unnecessary spending and regulations, and brought down inflation (the latter thanks to a tight money policy engineered by Fed Chairman Paul Volcker).

Our economic problems today are very different from those we faced in 1980, but an economic policy based on sound conservative principles will succeed this time around as well—if we have the political courage to end the dominance of Wall Street financiers and private-equity moguls over the American economy, while putting Main Street producers and small businessmen back in the driver's seat.

The hardest part in formulating an overall strategy to get our country back on the right track is figuring out how to restore our traditional beliefs. If ever our nation needed a strong moral compass, it is now. Witness the case of the $50 billion Ponzi scheme run by hedge-fund manager Bernard Madoff, which financially devastated many investors and charitable institutions. For far too long, we have simply taken it for granted that our Christian principles would remain the guiding light of our society. But our deep sense of family, neighborhood, community, a solid work ethic, and a strong faith in God has been severely weakened through the savage attacks on those values that began in earnest with the 1960's counterculture.

The emphasis on rights ("If it feels good, do it") rather than responsibilities, and a sense of entitlement rather than an understanding of obligation, have taken a heavy toll on the moral fabric of our society. Christianity is banned from the public square, criticism of homosexual behavior is viewed as a "hate crime," and a right to take the life of the innocent unborn is manufactured out of whole cloth by the highest court in our land.

It will be extraordinarily difficult to undo the damage done by hedonism and the Wall Street adaptation of Social Darwinism. Even Ronald Reagan did not have much success on the cultural front during his eight years in the White House, and he was the last president to try to make a difference in the Culture War. Still, the road to a cultural renaissance is there if we have the will to follow it.

Our country was not founded on the egalitarian, antireligious principles of the French Revolution. Our Founding Fathers knew that liberty was inseparable from a belief in God and obedience to divine law. George Carey, my political-theory professor at Georgetown University, notes this foundation of the American political tradition by pointing to the first words of the Mayflower Compact, written by the Pilgrims before they even got off the boat: "In the Name of God, Amen." William Penn, the founder of Pennsylvania, put the matter rather plainly: "Those who refuse to govern themselves by the laws of God will be ruled by tyrants."

The principles of right and wrong, an informed conscience, ordered liberty, the natural law, the Christian ethic—these guided us to greatness as a nation for nearly two hundred years and can do so again.

A New Strategy to Address

the Threat of Militant Islam

American foreign policy is in a shambles. The United States was the leader of the free world and the most-respected nation on the earth after the collapse of the Soviet Empire and the tearing down of the Cold War's most powerful symbol, the Berlin Wall. When Islamic extremists launched their suicide attacks against us on September 11, 2001, virtually the entire non-Muslim world rallied in support of the United States.

Instead of keeping our focus on the Islamic radical movement led by Osama bin Laden and attempting to diminish its influence within the broader Muslim community, the Bush administration stuck its hand into the beehive of Middle Eastern politics by invading Iraq. A preemptive war to remove from power the bloody secular dictator of Iraq, Saddam Hussein, was launched by President Bush at the urging of Vice President Dick Cheney and the President's neoconservative policy advisors, all in the name of the "War on Terror."

While Saddam Hussein was a ruthless dictator, he had nothing to do with the September 11 attacks. Indeed, the Iraqi leader was a bitter foe of Osama bin Laden.

The decision to go to war in Iraq wrought a profound change in the world's attitude toward the United States. We are now more isolated from, and less respected by, foreign nations. With the singular exception of Great Britain, our former European allies broke with us over the war. Now that Tony Blair is gone, even England is withdrawing its forces from Iraq. A poll conducted by Eurobarometer for the European Commission found that more than two thirds of the citizens of all 15 European Union countries see the war in Iraq as "not justified."

Countries that have a stake in diminishing the influence of

militant Islam were confused and baffled by the foreign policy of the Bush administration. Former Arkansas governor Mike Huckabee, a Republican presidential candidate in 2008, was on the mark when he wrote in *Foreign Affairs* that "the Bush administration's arrogant bunker mentality has been counterproductive both at home and abroad." Huckabee was also right to suggest that "American foreign policy needs to change its tone and attitude, open up, and reach out."

Eight years after the September 11 attacks, it is time to rethink our strategy for dealing with this latest challenge to Western civilization—one that is an even greater threat to our way of life than that posed by international communism in the 20th century.

Our current strategy for combating radical Islam is playing into Osama bin Laden's hands by radicalizing the Muslim population and uniting the Islamic world against us. By our actions, we are providing more foot soldiers for radical Islam.

The advocates of preemptive war in Iraq like to associate their strategy with the actions taken by the Reagan administration to defeat the Soviet Empire. Yet we won the Cold War with hardly a shot being fired by American forces and with relatively little loss of life. James Mann, author of the book *Rise of the Vulcans: The History of Bush's War Cabinet*, notes important distinctions between Ronald Reagan's foreign policy and that of the George W. Bush administration:

> The Iraq war underscores the first and most important difference between the two presidents: Mr Reagan was extremely cautious about sending troops into conflict. His military intervention in Grenada was small-scale and quick; when American marines were killed in Lebanon, he reacted by quickly withdrawing the troops. The ideas that eventually became known as the "Powell doctrine" for the use of force—that US forces should be sent to war only under limited circumstances, on a carefully defined mission, in overwhelming numbers and with a clear understanding of how the conflict will end—were originally drafted in 1984 by Caspar Weinberger, defense secretary, for Mr Reagan. (Weinberger's military aide at the time was Colin Powell, who then embraced and updated Weinberger's rules when he became chairman of the Joint Chiefs of Staff.)

It was precisely these Reagan-era rules that the present Bush administration cast aside in going to war in Iraq.... Second, in foreign policy, Mr Reagan, in spite of his truculent rhetoric, took care not to rule out dialogue with adversaries.... Third, as a politician Mr Reagan courted bipartisan support from the start of his administration. The thrust of his strategy was to win over Democrats in Congress, not humiliate them or draw partisan lines, as Mr Bush has.

One can put together an effective strategy to deal with the threat of militant Islam that does not feature the use of military force in the Middle East as the primary option. The principles of prudence and just-war theory should guide us.

It is worthwhile to review what transpired when U.S. troops were sent to Lebanon in 1982. The following summary is drawn from a study by the Wesleyan College Department of Government entitled "The US Marines in Lebanon."

Secretary of State George Schultz persuaded President Reagan to send a contingent of U.S. Marines to Lebanon in September 1982 as part of a multinational peacekeeping force. That decision was made over the objections of Secretary of Defense Caspar Weinberger and the Joint Chiefs of Staff, who were concerned about the "ambiguous nature of the mission" in a region in the Middle East that was in the throes of a civil war. Withdrawn less than 30 days later and then redeployed to Lebanon after the assassination of Lebanese President Bashir Gemayel, the Marines proved a sitting target for the Shiite suicide bomber who killed 241 of them on October 23, 1983, when he crashed his Mercedes truck loaded with explosives into the Marine barracks near the Beirut airport. The American troops standing guard at the barracks were not allowed to have ammunition in their weapons. They reported that, as the suicide bomber crashed through the gate, "he was smiling."

The bombing ignited a heated debate within the Reagan administration. Secretary of State Schultz and National Security Advisor Bud McFarlane wanted to send more troops into Lebanon and make a long-term military commitment. Secretary Weinberger and our military leaders warned that such a decision would get us bogged down in a war in the Middle East while diverting our attention from our primary mission of defeating the Soviet Empire. President Reagan ultimately sided with his secretary of defense. The President ordered the Marines withdrawn in early 1984.

Ronald Reagan himself later said that his greatest policy mistake was the sending of Marines to Lebanon:

> Perhaps we didn't appreciate fully enough the depth of the hatred and the complexity of the problems that make the Middle East such a jungle. Perhaps the idea of a suicide car bomber committing mass murder to gain instant entry to Paradise was so foreign to our own values and consciousness that it did not create in us the concern for the marines' safety that it should have. Perhaps we should have anticipated that members of the Lebanese military whom we were trying to assist would simply lay down their arms and refuse to fight their own countrymen. In any case, the sending of the marines to Beirut was the source of my greatest regret and my greatest sorrow as president. Every day since the death of those boys, I have prayed for them and their loved ones.

One of the few Republicans to argue against the President's decision to send American troops into Lebanon was freshman Congressman John McCain. He spoke forcefully against the move in September 1983 on the floor of Congress:

> The fundamental question is: What is the United States' interest in Lebanon? It is said we are there to keep the peace. I ask, what peace? It is said we are there to aid the government. I ask, what government? It is said we are there to stabilize the region. I ask, how can the U.S. presence stabilize the region? . . . The longer we stay in Lebanon, the harder it will be for us to leave. We will be trapped by the case we make for having our troops there in the first place.
> What can we expect if we withdraw from Lebanon? The same as will happen if we stay. I acknowledge that the level of fighting will increase if we leave. I regretfully acknowl-

edge that many innocent civilians will be hurt. But I firmly believe this will happen in any event.

While Ronald Reagan regretted his decision to send Marines into Lebanon, John McCain went from being a critic of putting U.S. troops into the Middle East to being the most vocal Republican advocate in Congress for using the U.S. military to "stabilize" various regions of the world. McCain supported the Clinton administration's war against Serbia and intervention in Kosovo on behalf of the Islamic Kosovo Liberation Army. He was a major proponent of the preemptive war in Iraq, and he has stated that the United States may need to keep troops there for up to 100 years. He has voiced support for the neoconservative goal of forcing regime change in Iran by bombing that nation's nuclear facilities. On the 2008 presidential campaign trail, McCain even sang the words "bomb bomb bomb, bomb bomb Iran" to an old Beach Boys tune.

It is hard to understand how the John McCain of the early 1980's, who saw the dangers of the United States getting sucked into an ambiguous military mission in the Middle East, could become the leading Republican proponent in Congress of a muscular military presence in the Middle East. This is not a policy direction Ronald Reagan would have followed.

After the bombing of the Marine barracks, the Reagan administration adopted a set of principles "to guide America in the application of military force abroad." It is too bad that George W. Bush did not apply these principles when deciding whether to go to war with Iraq:

1.   The United States should not commit its forces to military action overseas unless the cause is vital to our national interest.

2.   If the decision is made to commit our forces to combat abroad, it must be done with the clear intent and support needed to win. It should not be a halfway or tentative commitment, and there must be clearly defined and realistic objectives.

3.   Before we commit our troops to combat, there must be

reasonable assurance that the cause we are fighting for and the actions we take will have the support of the American people and Congress. (We all felt that the Vietnam War had turned into such a tragedy because military action had been undertaken without sufficient assurances that the American people were behind it.)

4.   Even after all these other tests are met, our troops should be committed to combat abroad only as a last resort, when no other choice is available.

President Reagan was very cautious about putting our soldiers in harm's way unless he deemed it to be in our national interest to do so—and only after he was sure that our military mission was clearly defined.

Our military intervention in Grenada fit these criteria. Shortly after the end of our military involvement in Lebanon, the President gave the order to send our forces into the Caribbean nation of Grenada to rescue U.S. medical students trapped in that communist-controlled country. On October 23 and 24, 1983, right after the Beirut bombing, American soldiers brought our students safely home while toppling the communist regime of Maurice Bishop, the head of the "New Jewel" revolutionary junta. The use of American troops in that situation turned out to be much more effective than the deployment of our Marines to Lebanon in pursuit of an uncertain mission in the Middle East.

Reagan's strategy to win the Cold War was a broad-based approach that incorporated political, economic, military, and spiritual elements designed to put pressure on the Soviet Empire and its satellites in key regions of the world—Eastern Europe, Afghanistan, and Central America. The Reagan administration generally used surrogates in those regions to undermine Soviet influence around the world. President Reagan also forged close alliances with world leaders, such as Pope John Paul II and Margaret Thatcher, who were as determined as he to roll back the tide of communism. People underestimate the importance of the spiritual dimension. The role of the Polish pope in the unraveling of the Soviet Empire in Eastern Europe and in the diminishing influence of the "Christian Marxists" in Central America was a critical component of an overall strategy designed to topple the "Evil Empire." This was particularly exemplified by the fall of communism in Poland.

All of these elements of a winning strategy—political, economic, military, and spiritual—must be woven together effectively if we are to defeat the forces of radical Islam. Our foe is formidable, and its goal is nothing less than world domination through the imposition of militant Islamic regimes around the globe.

The strategic threat is militant Islam, not "terror." We are engaged in a religious war, not because we wish it to be so, but because our enemies have defined it in those terms. For that reason alone, the spiritual component of our overall strategy becomes even more important.

A serious strategy to combat resurgent Islam must include repairing our badly damaged relationships with those nations that should be with us in this battle—nations that are just as threatened as we are (if not more so).

Western Europe is a good place to start that process of rebuilding alliances. The once-Christian (but now generally secular) nations of Europe have significant Muslim minorities in their midst. Nothing gets the attention of the majority of Europeans more quickly than the prospect of their children or grandchildren having to live under *sharia*, Islamic law. Demographics alone make that likely—perhaps in just two generations—even without a violent confrontation on European soil. Most Europeans are having fewer children while Muslim immigrants living in Europe typically have large families, just like their parents did in their homelands. It is significant that Mohammed was the most popular baby name for boys born in London in 2007.

Europeans are not unaware of the serious threat posed by militant Islam in their own backyard. In Germany, for example, three of the four September 11 hijackers (including one of the suspected masterminds) had been residents of Hamburg. There were only a few thousand Muslims residing in Germany at the end of World War II; there are now some 3.2 million. The French have their own problems with radicalized Muslims in their midst, and French authorities have responded toughly in dealing with suspected Islamic terrorists. The French also know what it is like to be a Western power occupying an Islamic country. The 1966 film *The Battle of Algiers* could serve as a training film for Muslims, illustrating how the Algerians drove the French out of their country.

Europeans have lived with the reality of militant Islam from long before we Americans even realized Islam might pose a threat to our way of life. When Europe was still a Christian civilization, it repelled the forces of Islam at the Battle of Lepanto. Christian historian Hilaire Belloc wrote that Islam

> failed during the last years of the seventeenth century. Vienna ... was almost taken and only saved by the Christian army under the command of the King of Poland on a date that ought to be among the most famous in history—September 11th, 1683. But the peril remained, Islam was still immensely powerful within a few marches of Austria and it was not until the great victory of Prince Eugene at Zenta in 1697 and the capture of Belgrade that the tide really turned—and by that time we were at the end of the seventeenth century.

In his prophetic work *The Great Heresies*, Belloc warned Europeans in the 1930's of the future strategic threat posed by a revitalized Islam:

> "Will not perhaps the temporal power of Islam return and with it the menace of an armed Mohammedan world which will shake off the domination of Europeans—still nominally Christian—and reappear again as the prime enemy of our civilization?" The future always comes as a surprise but political wisdom consists in attempting at least some partial judgment of what that surprise may be. And for my part I cannot but believe that a main unexpected thing of the future is the return of Islam. Since religion is at the root of all political movements and changes and since we have here a very great religion physically paralyzed but morally intense-

ly alive, we are in the presence of an unstable equilibrium which cannot remain permanently unstable.

We need to develop a coordinated strategic plan in conjunction with our European allies to target and isolate Islamic militants. Rather than go it alone, let's work with those forces in Europe that are willing to stand up to the threat of militant Islam.

In *Suicide of the West*, James Burnham described the inability of modern liberalism to respond effectively to the threat posed by international communism. Our secular leftist culture is equally incapable of responding to the challenge of Islam. Srdja Trifkovic defined the problem well in an article in the April 2007 issue of *Chronicles: A Magazine of American Culture*:

> A deeper malaise is at work. The real madness is an amorphous beast with many names—multiculturalism, one-worldism, tolerantism, inclusivism, antidiscriminationism—that demands engagement abroad and wide-open doors at home. Both abroad and at home, the impulse is neurotic; its justification, Gnostic. It reflects the collective loss of nerve, faith, and identity of a diseased society, producing a self-destructive malaise that is literally unprecedented in history.

That is why Pope Benedict's call for the re-Christianization of Europe is such a necessary part of any strategy to address the Islamic threat. As Theodore Dalrymple has written,

> Whatever else may be said of fierce Muslims, they are definitely not nihilists. They are not relativists either. They believe they are in possession of the truth, one and indivisible. For them, compromise is at best a mere tactic or a temporary truce until the balance of forces changes, as they now believe it will—entirely in their favor. Putting up Church of England clerics against them is like sending a 70-year-old into the ring to fight Mike Tyson in his prime.

As if to confirm Dalrymple's words, the archbishop of Canterbury, Rowan Williams, spoke in early 2008 about the "inevitability" of the introduction of *sharia* in England.

Other religious leaders, however, are up to the challenge. Russian Orthodox Bishop Hilarion Alfeyev is one. In a speech to an ecumenical Christian conference in Geneva, Bishop Hilarion espoused a more robust Christianity than that articulated by the archbishop of Canterbury:

> What has happened with Christianity? In a confused and disoriented world, where is the prophetic voice of Christians? . . . It is not our duty to defend sharia, promote alternative lifestyles or secularized values. Our mission is to announce what Christ himself announced . . . Liberal Christianity will not survive long, and political correctness within the Christian environment is destined to die.

The Balkans have historically been the gateway for Islamic attempts to overrun the Christian West. The Clinton administration made a major strategic mistake in supporting the radical Islamic KLA against the Christian Serbs who had been our allies in World War II. President Clinton's neoliberal foreign policy advisors, in particular Secretary of State Madeleine Albright and Assistant Secretary of State Richard Holbrooke, persuaded President Clinton to intervene militarily. Secretary of State Albright bluntly asked Gen. Colin Powell (who, as chairman of the Joint Chiefs of Staff, was reluctant to send U.S. troops into the Balkans), "What's the point of having this superb military that you're always talking about if we can't use it?" And so we used it to bomb Belgrade and other areas of Serbia while ensuring the Islamic takeover of Kosovo. The neoconservative proponents of the subsequent war in Iraq—Richard Perle, Paul Wolfowitz, Bill Kristol—were just as enthusiastic as the neoliberals in the Clinton administration in supporting the U.S. intervention in the Balkans. Most traditional conservatives opposed U.S. military action. When the neoconservative leaders decided to support the bombing of Serbia, I finally realized that the political philosophy they espoused was not conservatism and broke ranks with my former allies.

We also need to repair our badly damaged relationship with Russia, a natural ally in combating the threat of militant Islam. Russia is even more acutely aware of the dangers inherent in the rise of Islamic radicalism than the nations of Western Europe are. Russia faces her own internal Islamic threat in Chechnya and several other border regions. In addition, Russia has grave concerns about the emergence of an independent Kosovo dominated by the KLA. As retired Adm. James Lyons notes, the KLA commanders "have known ties to the global jihad movement and organized crime." Former CIA counterterrorism officer Philip Giraldi says that the predominantly Muslim state of Kosovo "harbors more than its share of terrorists, drug dealers, and weapons smugglers."

Russia and the United States have much in common, most notably our shared Christian faith. Even after eight decades, Soviet authorities were not able to stamp out the Christian faith of the Russian people. That is not to deny that communist rule wrought great spiritual harm on Russian society and on the culture of the Russian people, but the Russian Orthodox Church appears to be making a comeback. Even many Russian political leaders today publicly profess Orthodoxy.

A re-Christianized Russia may become our most important ally in the battle against militant Islam. I say this as a longtime conservative who was called "an outmoded Cold Warrior" by the communist propaganda newspaper *Izvestia* after I wrote an article critical of the Soviet regime for *U.S. News & World Report* back in 1971, and as a former Reagan administration official who was an unwavering supporter of President Reagan's policy to defeat the Soviet Empire. My opposition to Soviet communism, however, never made me anti-Russian any more than my opposition to Nazism would have caused me to become anti-German. In fact, one of the greatest prophetic voices of the 20th century, who challenged the communist regime with his remarkable writings about the Soviet Gulag, was a Russian named Aleksandr Solzhenitsyn. In his last Western interview before he returned to Russia, Solzhenitsyn told *Forbes* in April 1994: "One can see a time in the 21s century when both Europe and the U.S. will be in dire need of Russia as an ally."

The need for better relations with Russia seems so obvious to me that I am baffled by the constant attacks on Russia by neoconservative and neoliberal foreign-policy "experts." Vice President Cheney went out of his way to insult Russian leaders and treat their government like an enemy. It is hard to fathom how this could foster a decent working relationship in dealing with the threat we both face from a resurgent Islam.

Vladimir Putin is no angel; he was a longtime KGB agent before rising to power after the fall of the Soviet Empire. What did Putin inherit when he took over the Russian presidency from Boris Yeltsin? The country was in economic chaos. Yeltsin surely did not help matters by allowing a group of Russian oligarchs to loot the country of its natural resources, enriching themselves while leaving the Russian people impoverished.

When Putin came to power, he ended the rule of Russia by the oligarchs. The most notable member of the oligarchy was Russian billionaire Boris Berezovsky, who has been accused in *Forbes* magazine and other business publications of amassing his wealth through murder, fraud, and money-laundering. Berezovsky now lives in London, where he is plotting the overthrow of the Russian government.

One does not have to be supporter of Putin to be impressed with what his government has done to rebuild the Russian economy and to increase the incomes of the average Russian.

Putin also accomplished the restoration of the Russian Orthodox Church in Russian public life through his close working relationship with the late Russian Orthodox Patriarch Alexy II. As the leader of the Russian Orthodox believers, Alexy was a forceful and effective advocate for the re-Christianization of Europe. In December 2006, the patriarch delivered a stern warning to the West: "If European nations abandon their Christian roots, they are doomed to disappear from the historical arena. Modern Europe will not create a new post-Christian culture and civilization but will simply vanish from history . . . Losing their Christian roots, the people of Europe will sign their own death warrant."

Perhaps the threat of a resurgent Islam will motivate Russia and the United States to work together to develop Russia's abundant energy resources. Such an effort should aim to make more oil and gas available to Europe and the United States as we seek to decrease our reliance on unstable sources of fossil fuel in the Middle East.

Putin's Russia has been more prescient than the Bush administration in recognizing the dangers of creating an independent Islamic nation in the Balkans, an historic battleground in Islamic attempts to overrun Christian Europe. The history of Islamic intrusions into the Balkans has not been forgotten by Patriarch Alexy II, either. He has noted that Kosovo is "sacred land" to the Christian Serbs, though most Serbs in Kosovo have been forced to flee their homes because of Islamic aggression.

If we want to heal our rift with the Russians, we could start by changing our policy in the Balkans. Russia has a far more sensible view about that part of the world than U.S. policymakers do. The Serbs were our allies in World War II. They are fellow Christians who historically have been a bulwark against Islamic attempts to overrun Europe. Yet the Bush administration recognized Kosovo's declaration of independence in 2008 over Serbian and Russian objections. That recognition flies in the face of international law and is yet another strategic blunder of the Bush administration in our ongoing battle with militant Islam. In addition to Russia, a number of European nations, including Cyprus, Slovakia, Rumania, and Spain, protested Kosovo's illegal declaration of independence.

This is not to condone the atrocities that are alleged by either side in that conflict. War crimes, genocide, and ethnic violence of all forms should be condemned, and neither side has clean hands. But the fact remains that we did not act in our strategic national interest or with an understanding that the Balkans have historically been a gateway for Islamic incursions into Europe.

As we seek to develop a better working relationship with Russian leaders, we should have no illusions about the problems of Russian society. Russia still has a long way to go before she fully recovers her moral compass. The cancerous effects of eight decades of communist rule have not been undone in twenty short years. In late 2007, Solzhenitsyn pointed out that Russia's "domestic spiritual and moral atmosphere is far from being ideal." Before his death, he spoke of the urgent need for "spiritual development" in Russia. Nonetheless, as Russia proceeds through what he called this "very complex spiritual process," her interests in minimizing the influence of radical Islam mirror our own.

Another necessary change in our current policy concerns our official position on Turkey's entry into the European Union. Again, neoconservative and neoliberal foreign-policy advisors in the Clinton, Bush, and now Obama administrations have pressured Western European nations to admit Turkey (where militant Islamic influence has increased dramatically in recent years) into the European Union. That would lead to additional waves of Muslim immigrants washing across Western Europe. Muslims in Western Europe have large families and are growing rapidly as a percentage of the population in Western Europe, while Europeans continue to commit demographic suicide by not reproducing at replacement levels.

We should side with those European nations who oppose Turkey's entry into the European Union.

In Africa, where battles rage in a number of nations between Christian and Muslim forces, we should do what we did in the Reagan administration, when the CIA and the Department of Defense provided support to surrogate forces engaged in resisting communism. In this case, we would lend that support to the forces resisting Islamic expansion.

We should use our bully pulpit to speak up for the rights of Christian minorities in various Arab countries. Our foreign-policy leaders should quietly inform the Saudi rulers that it is no longer acceptable for them to subsidize the expansion of their brand of radical Islam abroad. Cynics might say that this financial support helps the oligarchy stay in power in Saudi Arabia, but it is doing great harm by fueling an extremist Islamic ideology around the globe.

Sending American soldiers into war is one of the most difficult decisions any president of the United States has to make. Young Americans should be sent off to war only when our national interest is clearly at stake, the mission is carefully defined, and the American people authorize the president to take that action by a congressional declaration of war. Such a national "seal of approval" will carry the country through the hard times that arise during war without causing painful divisions among the people.

Sen. Robert Taft said that the purpose of American foreign policy was the "maintenance of the liberty and peace of the people of the United States." With that in mind, it makes sense to withdraw our Armed Forces from Iraq as quickly as possible under the circumstances. We also need to consider the economic consequences of our massive expenditures in Iraq. Again, Senator Taft has words of wisdom on that subject: "We can assume a financial burden in our foreign policy so great that it threatens liberty at home."

General Powell was right when he said that "once you break the vase, you own it." It was a strategic mistake to launch a preemptive war against Iraq. But it is a lot harder to get out of Iraq with honor than it was to go there in the first place. We need to turn to those with extensive experience in the Middle East (like retired Gen. Anthony Zinni, an original critic of the war) to guide us in constructing a strategy for withdrawing from Iraq. (It is unfortunate that someone in the Obama administration torpedoed the nomination of General Zinni to be ambassador to Iraq.)

Once our withdrawal from Iraq is accomplished, we must put our badly overextended military back together again. The Army has had to lower its standards repeatedly in order to meet recruiting goals, at a much higher cost per recruit than ever before. Our military reserves and National Guard were never intended to serve multiple tours in foreign war zones. Nor can we keep sending our regular soldiers on multiple tours of duty to Iraq and Afghanistan. We are simply wearing our soldiers out.

It was disturbing to read in the October 2007 issue of *VFW* magazine that "Army suicides hit 26-year high." The report cited in the article showed "that a soldier was more likely to attempt suicide if he or she had served more than one tour in a war zone." We cannot treat our soldiers like pawns in a chess match, as our civilian armchair generals in Washington, D.C., have been wont to do.

The National Guard is much more suited to deal with disasters and national emergencies here at home. We need to bring the Guard home from these foreign countries as soon as possible. And, once they are home, we must keep them here, where, among other things, they can play an important role in securing our borders.

Most Americans agree on the need to secure our borders. But there is little public discussion about the importance of rewriting our immigration laws to restrict immigration from countries with predominantly Islamic populations. Srdja Trifkovic, author of *The Sword of the Prophet*, calls our immigration policy "suicidal" on that score. The United States "granted 100,000 green cards in 2005 alone" to Muslim immigrants. Beyond simple restriction, we also need to change our laws to permit profiling of possible terrorist suspects. We profile serial killers. We should profile those who are most likely to commit acts of violence like those of September 11. We need to repeal our so-called anti-discrimination laws, which prohibit companies in sensitive positions from screening out potential hires who might pose a security risk. And those already in the United States who advocate *jihad* should be returned to the country from which they came.

While forcefully opposing radical Islam at home and abroad, the United States should have a more balanced policy in the Middle East, in the interest of both justice and common sense. We do not need to drive more Muslims into the radical camp. The worst-kept secret in Washington, D.C., is that the United States backs Israel to the hilt on every major issue in the Middle East—even when the Israeli government is wrong and shortsighted in its thinking. Gen. Brent Scowcroft, director of the National Security Council under George H.W. Bush, told the *Financial Times* that our policy in the Middle East became far too one-sided during the George W. Bush presidency. The United States is no longer considered an honest broker in the Middle East. This was not the case when Presidents Jimmy Carter, Ronald Reagan, George H.W. Bush, and Bill Clinton were in office. Those presidents pursued a balanced policy in the Middle East while simultaneously maintaining our close ties to Israel.

Our own national interests should be our highest priority. The national interests of the United States and Israel are often similar, but not always. The United States needs to reestablish a more independent foreign policy in the Middle East and become less subservient to the policy agenda of the American Israel Public Affairs Committee, the most powerful foreign-policy lobby in Washington, D.C., today.

Of course, in the long run, a more balanced policy in the

Middle East will help diminish the influence of Islamic radicalism and be beneficial to Israel as well.

The failures of American foreign policy during the Clinton and George W. Bush administrations illustrate the dictum that "personnel make policy." Neoliberals such as Madeleine Albright and Richard Holbrooke persuaded Bill Clinton to support the Islamic KLA against the Christian Serbs. Neoconservatives Paul Wolfowitz, Douglas Feith, Lewis "Scooter" Libby, Richard Perle, and John Bolton (among others) were the architects of the George W. Bush administration's war in Iraq, and their principal sponsor was Vice President Dick Cheney.

Ronald Reagan was able to change our failed foreign policy against communism by bringing a group of outsiders with him to Washington, D.C., to implement his strategy. Bill Casey at the CIA, Bill Clark at the National Security Council, and Cap Weinberger at the Department of Defense were the key figures in the execution of the Reagan strategy, and none of them were part of the New York/ Washington foreign-policy establishment.

Any president who is serious about changing the direction of American foreign policy and adopting a more realistic strategy to combat radical Islam needs to bring his own foreign-policy team with him. In the case of a conservative president, there should be no neoconservative or neoliberal ideologues in that number. Both groups of foreign-policy "experts" have led us into the mess we are in today. We should not reward failure by putting the same old crowd of retreads back in charge of running American foreign policy. There are plenty of capable Americans out there—Goldwater/Reagan conservatives, retired military leaders, ex-CIA officials, and former State Department personnel—who understand the need for a change in the direction of our foreign policy and who would gladly step forward to serve in any administration that adopts a less utopian and more realistic strategy to address the threat of global *jihad*.

Putting America Back to Work

*"The budget should be balanced, the Treasury should be refilled,
public debt should be reduced, the arrogance of officialdom
should be tempered and controlled, and the assistance
to foreign lands should be curtailed lest Rome become bankrupt.
People must again learn to work, instead of living on public assistance."*
~attributed to Tullius Cicero

The first step in revitalizing the American economy is to put Main Street back in charge of corporate America. The "new capitalism" we are living under now is a far cry from the free-market system that made America great. A writer in the *Financial Times* (June 19, 2007) described the salient features of that "new capitalism": "We have the triumph of the global over the local, of the speculator over the manager, and the financier over the producer."

During the 2008 presidential primaries, former Arkansas governor Mike Huckabee caught a lot of flack from Washington Beltway Republicans and the Wall Street crowd for arguing that the Republican Party and the conservative movement needed to return to their small-business, middle-class roots. Yet that's what Barry Goldwater and Ronald Reagan stood for when they ran for president.

Why should our economy be dominated by Wall Street financial engineers and private-equity moguls rather than Main Street producers?

Sen. Barry Goldwater, the Republican presidential nominee in 1964, led a political movement that represented the "forgotten Americans," the middle-class taxpayers who did not have a lobbyist in Washington and weren't looking for loopholes in the law. Goldwater contrasted his philosophy of Main Street conservatism with the corporate liberalism of the Rockefeller Republicans of Wall Street. He warned of the dangers of too much power being concentrated in the hands of Big Business, Big Labor, and Big Government

151

to the detriment of the average citizen. The Goldwater conservative movement ultimately led to the election of Ronald Reagan as president in 1980. Yet in this post-Reagan era of American politics, Main Street conservatives have been relegated to the sidelines as Wall Street types, big-business corporate liberals, and Washington lobbyists have seized control of the Republican machinery.

So how do we put Main Street America back in charge?

We need to resist the advice of those economists who welcome a weakened U.S. dollar as the only way out of our unsustainable trade deficits. At the moment, their advice is being followed. In 2008, for the first time in decades, the Canadian dollar could buy more than the U.S. one, and the dollar was at its lowest value against the euro since that currency came into existence. The decline in our currency continued in 2009, while gold has held up strongly during this period against all paper currencies, including the dollar. How long can the dollar maintain its value, given the trillions of dollars in federal debt run up through the Bush-Obama stimulus packages? And who will buy all of our additional paper at today's low interest rates?

Inflation is running at a much higher rate than the official Consumer Price Index (CPI), which underweights the cost of food, energy, housing, and healthcare in its statistical formula. Real inflation in the United States was running anywhere from seven to ten percent in late 2007. We have only to look at the examples of the German Weimar Republic and Argentina at various stages of her history to see what can happen when a debased currency spirals out of control and loses most of its value. You destroy your middle class and your economy.

To make the dollar sound and worth something again, we have to institute a tough fiscal policy at the national level. We cannot spend money we don't have and should not initiate programs we cannot afford. Our nation must live within its means. We have to learn to "just say no."

Piecemeal measures will not suffice. Serious policy changes need to be made quickly to restore a sound dollar, because a sound dollar is fundamental to a sound economy. We have defied every conservative, constitutional principle of government and pretended that the bill would not come due someday.

Our trade deficits are huge because we have turned the principles of a sound economy upside down—our business tax system rewards high levels of corporate debt while penalizing savings and investment here at home.

The combination of out-of-control government spending and a fatally flawed tax policy is lethal. The facts are staring us in the face: We cannot expect other nations to continue lending us $2.5 billion a day to keep our economy afloat—especially when they lose money in the process as the dollar declines in value. In this global economy, there are far more stable and attractive investments for foreign investors than buying our government paper.

Lenin's timeless question confronts us: "What is to be done?" The most honest and prudent approach is as simple as it is difficult: Our country has to rethink the way our government spends our money. And we need to figure out a way to level the playing field with our trading partners and stop the steady loss of good-paying manufacturing jobs to other nations.

The prospect of trillion-dollar trade and budget deficits for the next five to ten years is a dagger aimed at the heart not only of our economy, but of our way of life. The profligacy of the Bush and, now, the Obama years must come to an end. Merely "slowing the rate of growth" will not be sufficient to stop the bleeding of an economy in decline.

The Obama administration is even worse than the Bush administration when it comes to excessive spending. President Obama's proposed budget is the most massive ever, with a proposed deficit of nearly two trillion dollars for Fiscal Year 2010. As the *Financial Times* has noted, that is "equivalent to 12 per cent of gross domestic product (GDP) [with] . . . the gap between tax receipts and spending at its greatest since the second world war." Meanwhile, the U.S. economy contracted by 6.2 percent in the fourth quarter of 2008, the largest decline since 1982. The United States is facing "its worst economic downturn since the second world war," and the Obama stimulus package of nearly $800 billion had next to nothing in it to encourage job creation in the private sector. Government cannot spend its way out of this crisis.

The *Wall Street Journal* has said that the nation can learn from the Texas model of economic development: low taxes, fiscal restraint, and regulatory reform. Instead, the federal government seems hellbent on following the California model: high taxes, fiscal mismanagement, and regulatory overkill. To see the likely results, all we have to do is look at what's happening in California. To see what could happen if Washington adopted sane policies, we need only look at Texas.

California is struggling to overcome a budget deficit of more than $42.5 billion. In his State of the State address on January 15, 2009, Governor Schwarzenegger declared, "The truth is that California is in a state of emergency." The deficit "is a rock upon our chest and we cannot breathe until we get it off." According to CNN Money, the state was just "days away from not having enough money to cover all its bills." Governor Schwarzenegger's solution was to raise taxes on individuals and businesses by more than $12 billion and increase state bond debt. Even after raising taxes and cutting spending to address the $42.5 billion shortfall, California still found itself with an $8 billion deficit in the spring of 2009. Meanwhile, the main budgetary challenge facing Texas in 2009 was to avoid being tempted to overspend its budget surplus.

California cannot blame national and international problems for its financial woes. Jean Ross, executive director of the California Budget Project, admits that "California went into this downturn in a very weak position." Texas, on the other hand, can boast that its policies have cushioned external blows to its economy. The unemployment rate in Texas is more than a point below the national average and more than three points below the California rate. While the nation lost more than two million jobs between October 2007 and 2008, Texas was gaining more than 200,000 jobs because the state is known for being business-friendly, with low taxes, prudent spending at the state level, and fewer unnecessary regulations.

Texas has learned the most important lesson of job creation: Government cannot create jobs; only the private sector can. While the government may seem to create jobs when it hires people or buys things, it destroys at least as many jobs as it creates when it does so. It has to get the money to pay the people it hires from somewhere, and that somewhere will have that much less money to hire people and buy things. John Maynard Keynes, the intellectual founding father of deficit spending, said that he did not care whether the government paid some people to dig holes and other people to fill them in. Common sense tells us that such Keynesian ideas on how to dig ourselves out of a serious recession or depression are nonsensical, yet Keynesianism is making a comeback in the Obama administration.

A tax policy concocted by Wall Street financiers, globalists, and an army of special-interest lobbyists has led us to disaster. The quickest way to reduce our unsustainable trade deficits and rebuild our manufacturing base is to reform our business tax system along the lines recommended by Austin, Texas, business economist David Hartman. Mr. Hartman, the chairman of the Lone Star Foundation, has built a number of successful companies in manufacturing and financial services. Among his proposals for tax reform is an eight percent border-adjusted consumption tax. That tax, he estimates, would replace our current corporate income tax and reduce the estate tax (the infamous "death tax"), as well as fund a tax credit that would be applied against the employer's share of FICA taxes. This border-adjusted, value-added tax (VAT) would not apply to U.S. exports, but would be applied to all imports.

This change in tax policy would make the U.S. competitive by removing the advantage our trading partners enjoy as a result of the border-adjusted VATs they have put in place to help their domestic companies. This revenue-neutral change would also be much less of a burden on the U.S. economy. The VAT would allow for the expensing of fixed investment, eliminating double taxation of investment. This would result in an accelerated growth of savings and investment and create private-sector jobs. In the long run, the VAT would bring in a lot more money than the taxes it would replace, because the U.S. economy would grow much faster. We would have a tax system that would encourage companies to create jobs in the United States and keep them here.

The U.S. business tax code, with its high rate of 35 percent, encourages companies to send jobs overseas, move American manufacturing facilities to foreign countries, and take on high levels of debt in order to avoid taxes.

The Hartman proposal would reward U.S.-based businesses for corporate investment and savings in the United States and would end the punitive taxes imposed by our existing system. With this clearheaded, sensible reform, exports would increase significantly, and we would begin to rebuild our manufacturing base and lessen our dependence on foreign energy and imported consumer goods.

As Hartman points out, since the Industrial Revolution, manufacturing has been the leading source of competitive advantage in terms of income, wealth, and military strength. The restoration and preservation of our manufacturing sector is thus vital to our national interest. The adoption of a border-adjusted value-added tax is the first step toward such a restoration.

Hartman's tax proposal would also cut our soaring trade deficit in half and reinvigorate our middle class.

If Hartman's proposal were enacted, the financial engineers would no longer be in control of the American economy. American-based businesses would be encouraged to save and invest, and the tax advantages of heavy corporate debt would be gone. That would be good news for Americans workers, our manufacturing base, and shareholders in U.S. companies. Adopting a border-adjusted value-added tax would reduce the outsourcing of jobs, encourage long-term investment in U.S. companies, and put business owners back in charge of the American economy.

Providing businesses with a tax credit, funded from the VAT revenues, for the employer's share of FICA taxes would stimulate job creation in the United States. Conservatives have long set their sights on the inheritance tax, and for good reason. Reducing or getting rid of the inheritance tax would ensure that successful family businesses could be passed on to the next generation. Our current tax system forces many family businesses onto the auction block. After a taxpayer has paid taxes on all income and assets for a lifetime, inheritance taxation is pure confiscation from the family and lost long-term investment for the country.

Such a change in our economic policy could not come at a more critical time. The American middle class is disappearing. As

economist Martin Hutchison points out, "the declining share of low
and moderate income workers in the American pie is undeniable;
the relative share of such workers peaked as long ago as 1973. For
those with only high school qualifications or less, their absolute
earnings peaked in 1973 and have declined substantially since
then." Hutchison cites a Center for Economic and Policy Research
study which "shows that the share of 'good jobs' in the US economy
has fallen substantially during the 2001-07 business cycle, where a
'good job' was defined as one that pays at least $17 an hour (the
median wage rate in 1979) and offers employer-provided health
insurance and a pension." Hutchison calls for a "new intellectual
paradigm" to address this "impoverishment of the American middle
class." That is what the Hartman plan represents.

A border-adjusted value-added tax could win broad bipartisan
support—as well as support from corporate America and labor
unions. The only likely opponents to such reform are the foreign
nations that currently enjoy a huge trading advantage over us, the
Wall Street financiers and private equity funds that benefit from
the current tax system, and our domestic socialists who favor
high taxes on everyone with money and on all private businesses.
Since all of these special interests have powerful connections in
Washington, it will take a concerted, targeted effort to overcome
their opposition, but it would be worth the effort. The Hartman
plan offers us a concrete and achievable means to address immediately the most serious economic threats that we face.

The revitalization of our manufacturing sector is critical from
a national-security standpoint, as well as an economic one. Our
manufacturing superiority helped us win World War II and was a
key advantage over the Soviet Union during the Cold War.

There are ways to provide an economic "stimulus" without
deficit spending. We need to rekindle the American work ethic in
which individuals take pride in their work and in using the talents
God gave them. The early Obama policies are doing just the opposite, creating the expectation of handouts.

Give a man a fish, the proverb goes, and you'll feed him for a
day; teach a man to fish, and you'll feed him for a lifetime. That
was the message of Booker T. Washington to the students at the

Tuskegee Institute, which he founded in 1881 to educate freed slaves. Washington encouraged a strong work ethic among his students and emphasized self-improvement as a means to economic advancement and self-sufficiency.

Compare that with the socialist economic philosophy of Washington's rival for the leadership of the black community at the time. W.E.B. DuBois favored government solutions to the economic problems of the black community. President Obama seems to be listening more to the advice of W.E.B. DuBois than that of Booker T. Washington.

Building on the Booker T. Washington philosophy of self-sufficiency, our educational system must prepare students for real jobs in the real world with an emphasis on the skills that can help our young people become self-reliant.

Job creation in the private sector, along with a renewed emphasis on fundamental skills and a good work ethic: That is the kind of stimulus plan we need to put Americans back to work.

For years, I have been among those Americans warning about the dangers of a "pass the trash" mortgage system, in which mortgage originators can make questionable home loans and pay no price for their mistakes. In too many cases, mortgage originators put people in homes they could not afford. The mortgages were then handed off to financial institutions that packaged them, then turned around and sold them again. The originators are long gone, but financial institutions and investors at the end of the chain are stuck with "bad paper" while homeowners unable to make their payments lose their houses and have their credit ruined.

Why didn't our financial institutions see this coming? Historically, local financial institutions, primarily savings-and-loan associations, made mortgage loans and had to take the property back if the homeowners failed to make their payments. Thus the local lending institutions had every incentive to make sure (as best they could) that the borrower was credit-worthy, could afford the monthly payment, and that there was enough equity in the house to allow the lender to recover his principal if the loan went bad.

This was the old-fashioned way: It put the lender, as well as the borrower, on the hook. Both parties to the loan shared responsibility, and families made tremendous sacrifices to ensure they were able to make their mortgage payments and realize the American dream of home ownership. That all changed with the slick bundling of packages of mortgages by Wall Street financiers who sold them off to investors who had no way of knowing the quality of the original loans. Instead of a face-to-face relationship between borrower and lender, the mortgage evaporated into a cloud of impersonal financiers bent on making a killing. The house of cards fell hard in the summer of 2007.

Some suggest that the collapse was the result of falling home prices or too many "uncreditworthy borrowers," rather than credit excess. The data suggests otherwise. An IMF analysis of the subprime mortgage collapse found that the underlying cause was "excessive and inappropriate lending; rather than a growth in the proportion of fundamentally uncreditworthy borrowers." The IMF study reveals that the loan-to-value ratio in adjustable-rate mortgages (ARMs) climbed from 38 percent in 2003 to 56 percent in 2006. Over half of the subprime ARMs in 2006 had less than a ten-percent equity cushion built into the loan. And by 2006 only 53 percent of those who took out subprime mortgages provided full credit documentation to justify the loan.

There is a relatively simple solution to the "pass the trash" mortgage game. The market itself will correct many of the problems. But Dr. Jan Krahnen, a professor of economics at the University of Frankfurt, writing in the *Financial Times* (September 28, 2007), offers a commonsense solution to the abuses that the market cannot fix:

> The so-called first loss piece, or equity tranche, should be permanently held by the originator. The reason is moral hazard, or the risk of irresponsible lending . . . The lender must remain personally involved or, in financial terms, he must remain at risk by keeping a deductible. The retention of a first loss piece in a CDO (Collateralized Debt Obligation) transaction achieves exactly that.

In other words, if you originate the mortgage, you must remain at risk in the event the loan goes bad. Richard Portes, president of the Center for Economic Policy Research, echoes Krahnen, arguing that "governments should consider requiring financial houses that make loans and then sell them off as securities to retain some of the risk on their books to prevent a repeat of the current problems." Portes told the *Wall Street Journal* that the retained debt should be "enough to make it hurt if their product turns out to be a much lower value than the initial assessment suggests."

These rather simple changes to the mortgage process would clean up many of the abuses that arose under the "pass the trash" system.

Collateralized Debt Obligations are not the only ticking time bomb we face today. Warren Buffet has called Credit Default Swaps (CDSs) "weapons of mass financial destruction," and his own companies have suffered significant financial losses from their involvement in CDSs When Enron collapsed and went into bankruptcy, it was more a company that traded in derivatives than it was an energy company. AIG, which we think of as an insurance company, had become a company which sold credit derivatives. Gretchen Morgenson has an excellent explanation of derivatives in her March 8, 2009, article in the *New York Times* entitled "A.I.G., Where Taxpayers' Dollars Go to Die."

According to Morgenson, "Some $440 billion in credit default swaps sat on the company's books before it collapsed. Its biggest customers, European banks and United States investment banks, bought the swaps to insure against defaults on a variety of debt holdings, including pools of mortgages and corporate loans."

The big difference between Enron and AIG is that Enron was allowed to go into bankruptcy, while AIG was bailed out by the taxpayers. The counterparties on the other side of the Enron derivatives trades suffered substantial financial losses. But the AIG contracts on the CDSs "got bought out at par ... when they should have taken a hit," declared Eric Houde on CNBC (March 2, 2009).

Morgenson notes that Goldman Sachs was a leading counterparty on the credit-default swaps with AIG and that sitting in on the meeting to decide AIG's fate were Secretary of the Treasury Henry Paulson (former CEO of Goldman Sachs) and Lloyd Blankfein (chairman and CEO of Goldman at the time of the taxpayer bailout of AIG). Moreover, the man tapped to head AIG after the bailout was Edward Liddy, who served five years on the board of Goldman Sachs before resigning to become chairman and CEO of AIG.

Gretchen Morgenson explains what happened with the initial $85 billion bailout of AIG:

> The rescue of A.I.G. also involved a bailout of its many customers, none of whom the insurer or the government is willing to identify.
>
> Nevertheless, Edward M. Liddy, the chief executive of A.I.G., explained to investors last week that "the vast majority" of taxpayer funds "have passed through A.I.G. to other financial institutions" as the company unwound deals with its customers.
>
> On Wall Street, those customers are known as "counterparties," and Mr. Liddy wouldn't provide details on who the counterparties were or how much they received. But a person briefed on the deals said A.I.G.'s former customers include Goldman Sachs, Merrill Lynch and two large French banks, Société Générale and Calyon.
>
> All the banks declined to comment.
>
> How much money has gone to counterparties since the company's collapse? The person briefed on the deals put the figure at around $50 billion.

Hank Greenberg, former CEO of AIG, obviously had an ax to grind in his complaints about the U.S. takeover and bailout of AIG; but he was right that U.S. tax dollars should not have been used to make good the claims of the counterparties. "Christmas came early for many of them. It was a gift," Greenberg told the *Financial Times* (March 9, 2009).

Goldman Sachs received one hundred cents on the dollar (nearly $13 billion) in taxpayer money from AIG on its credit derivative trades with AIG. Merrill Lynch got $6.8 billion, while foreign banks such as Société Générale and Deutsche Bank got close to $12 billion—also paid by U.S. taxpayers.

Severe limitations need to be imposed on the derivative trading markets. Christine Harper of Bloomberg reported (March

7, 2009) that even Myron Scholes, an economist who invented a model for pricing options, has called on regulators "to blow up or burn over-the-counter derivative trading markets."

While trade in CDOs and CDSs is confined to banks and other financial institutions, another economic time bomb affects almost every adult American. Dallas money manager Pat Riddell estimates that five billion dollars' worth of credit-card solicitations are mailed out each year. Riddell reports that the average credit-card holder carries seven credit cards and owes approximately $10,000 in total credit-card debt. Unfortunately, many credit-card companies are nothing more than high-risk gamblers. They play a numbers game, offering credit cards with high interest rates, punitive late fees, and other penalties that can result in effective annual interest rates in excess of 30 percent. Today, millions of consumers are trapped in a vicious cycle of debt and are headed for bankruptcy. They scramble to find new cards that will keep them above water for another month or two, but eventually they fall hopelessly behind in their payments. The companies make their real money from those who pay late, not from those who behave like responsible customers. Financial laws allow this—and it turns the American dream upside down, since such companies have every reason to encourage credit-card holders to be irresponsible in their spending. No wonder our government is ten trillion dollars in debt—it's the same attitude, only on a grander scale. Unlike our government, however, the average credit-card holder cannot print his own money, and eventually he has to face the music. Meanwhile, the credit-card issuers rake in so much from their usurious fees that they can afford a "reasonable" rate of write-offs. So long as most debtors keep making at least partial payments, the companies will keep on making money.

Our slowing economy and the declining housing market have made home-equity loans—a popular way to refinance credit-card debt—much harder to obtain. Should the credit crunch worsen, we will be headed for a train wreck—and both credit-card companies and borrowers will turn out to be losers.

We would not have a credit-card-debt problem of this magnitude were it not for the federal preemption of state usury laws (limiting the interest rates lenders can charge). That preemption needs to be phased out over a reasonable period of time in order to lessen our dependence on personal credit.

Throughout the history of Western civilization, usury has been viewed as an unethical practice. Aristotle and Thomas Aquinas, among many great thinkers, wrote about the evils of usury. In my generation, we associated usury with the Mafia—and that's where it belongs.

For the long-term health of our economy and for the sake of consumers trapped in a seemingly endless cycle of credit-card debt, the usury laws need to be put back in place for the credit-card industry. Rates should be capped at 18 percent or less for all credit-card interest charges, along with other penalties. Arkansas is a worthy model to consider. In 1982, the state passed a constitutional amendment capping interest rates at five percent above the federal discount rate.

There were many good reasons for laws prohibiting unreasonably high interest rates. Usury needs to be made illegal again.

Of course, even if all of the structural changes to our economic system that I have proposed were implemented, they would not address the problem of the worst rising to the top so often in corporate America. Nonetheless, these economic reforms would make less influential those who practice usury and the asset-stripping of American businesses for short-term personal gain.

A free market only works if those who participate in it have a solid moral compass.

In his book *The New Legacy*, my good friend Skipper Dippel recounted his dying father's advice to him about the importance of preserving his good name and always treating others ethically. I cannot think of a better expression of business ethics. With Skipper's permission, I give you "One Father's Words":

> Now, I don't want you to worry about me. I will get over this as I have survived everything else. But just in case something unexpected should happen to me, I want you to take charge. Don't let the family dwell upon it. Time and life go on. I have been fortunate to be able to live my life as a lion.

163

Two weeks of that is worth a lifetime as a lamb.

I chose to keep our family in Brenham and Texas, rather than going to other places and trying new opportunities. That might have been more profitable, but Brenham still holds the values that first brought your great-grandfather to the states almost 100 years ago. Some of these values will change, but most will remain the same as they have throughout history. It is important to remember that no matter how they try in Congress, they cannot repeal the law of gravity. God's laws and natural laws are the ultimate power in this world. Some people may only discover them after a lifetime, but they do exist. Recognizing them is critical.

The most important thing I can leave you is a good name, and I think I have done that. Your mother and I have worked and saved a long time to create this beginning for you and your sister. Home has always been the most important part of our lives and should be yours. We hope we have taught you the importance of our values and passed along our heritage. You have an education that will help you achieve what is really important in life—being a responsible citizen, loving husband, and sensitive father. There may be more to living, but these three areas can make your life deeply satisfying.

What I feel I will be leaving you is an opportunity—a start from which you can make your own mark. The time that we spend on earth is relatively small in comparison with the great movement of history. All we can do within our life span is to make the world better than it was when we first arrived. All fortunes eventually are dispersed, but the ideas and values that you leave to society can live forever. I hope you and Kitty will have a wonderful family, just as your mother and I had with you and Deanna. Being a good father is your greatest challenge and responsibility. Teach your children the ideals you think are proper. Give them the best values that you can. And teach them how to judge what is best for their lives and nation. We must try to make every generation's character better than the one before it and build a higher standard of living through wise policies.

Don't underestimate the power and value of ideas, politics, and money. But never let any of these be your God. Learn to acquire and use them, but make absolutely certain that you understand the purposes for which they are being used.

Lots of things have changed in Texas since I was a young man, and they will continue to change even faster during the next 20 years as your generation assumes leadership. You will need to keep a clear sense of what's important. I remember hearing how my dad came to Texas from Germany. Whenever a family suffered a bad harvest or business disaster, their neighbors helped them out until they were able to get back on their feet again. Now it seems that everyone is out for his own piece of the pie regardless of who else starves. There is still charity, but people are sometimes too busy to hear their consciences. Too often even charity itself is commercialized; but if a dime out of each dollar reaches the needy, it is worth our efforts.

Life is already different from a few years ago. I am worried about the way politics is changing. People don't know their leaders personally. They don't seem to have the same respect as they did in my day for the ideas that made America strong. Texas can have a great impact on our country. But as Texans, we can either mature and bring our ideas to other Americans, or we can create a petty state that will be defeated by partisanship. If that happens, we will make little difference.

I have hoped that you and other young people can understand the changes occurring in politics and economics and how they affect you. Then you'll be able to handle them. In the process, you'll turn Texas and America in a more positive direction again.

Remember to associate with people who care more about whether they go to heaven or hell than whether they become governor of Texas or head of a company. Ambition can be your worst enemy. Often you are not a good leader until you have lost your ambition and come face to face with what is most important in life. Guard against both ambition

165

and pride, or in the long run you will be a loser, perhaps
not in appearance, but in reality. You will have to deal with
all types of people in life. Some will be genuine and others
not. It will be hard to judge them until you have had experience with them. Do not hesitate to cultivate friends because
that is what makes life enjoyable. However, watch new acquaintances for a while before giving them your trust.

One certainty in life is that you are not always on top.
There are many people who try to avoid the falls by changing philosophies. These are people of convenience. They're
often successful in the short term, while they are on earth.
But I have always wondered whether they were successful
in the sense of eternity. I feel following conscience is a far
better guide.

Remember to judge people on their merit and not
by their possessions or jobs. People should be judged by
how they use their success rather than by how much they
acquire. There is a difference between self-respect and
pride. Just as there always will be differences in abilities
and destinies, there always will be economic distinctions.
But we have a responsibility to allow people to keep their
self-respect. Your grandfather taught this to me early in life
when he took me to his wholesale grocery. The Depression
made life in Texas very tough, and few people made money.
Everyone helped his neighbors and enjoyed closeness and
cooperation. Your grandfather and I would slit open sacks
of flour and spend what seemed to be a lifetime trying to
crack, not break, some eggs. I thought this was one of the
most foolish things I had ever seen and could not understand why he would ruin good merchandise at a time when
everyone was losing money.

So he sat down with me, and we had a conversation that
I always will remember. He said his employees had helped
him build the business. They had gone through many hard
years together to make the business a success. They all
knew he couldn't afford to keep them on, but my dad felt
he had a responsibility to help. Dad said, "If you offer these

people money for doing nothing, some of them would not take it because they would lose their self-respect. Those who would accept the money would suffer equally from a loss of inner strength." So, I watched with admiration as my father offered damaged goods to his former employees in exchange for helping him move the merchandise.

The older you become, the more you'll recognize the importance of finding a purpose in life. But first you need to learn about reality. Emotion more than thought rules your life when you are a child. Ambition and ego guide your conscience more than responsibility. As your maturity and understanding develop, you'll think about mortality. Your thoughts will reach a deeper level of understanding. You will discover that God gave you freedom of choice in how you live your life. The most important thing you can do is to find a sense of love and oneness with God and other people. I became a better person when I learned the lessons of stewardship and how to deal with others by reading the Bible. In that way, I found my own meaning for life. You will go through a similar process as you question why you were put on this earth.

The rule of the world is not just to take from life, but to put something back. We all have responsibilities, although sometimes we would like to ignore them, especially the difficult ones. Some men can affect very little, but they still have the responsibility to do what they can in a positive way. I have tried to do that. On occasions I have been right and on others I've been wrong. When I was wrong, I was able to admit it. At least God knew my motives. That makes the later times of life, like these, a lot more satisfying.

There are many things you can learn from the Bible. The parable of the talents teaches you that all of us are judged by what we do with our resources. The more ability you are given, the more is expected of you. God has given you a number of abilities. Please don't waste them.

Reforming Our Educational System

We spend much more on education today than we did 50 years ago, and we have a lot less to show for it. We should have listened to the words of Sen. Barry Goldwater on the subject in his book *The Conscience of a Conservative*. He devoted an entire chapter to education, and his warnings about the dangers of federal control have been completely ignored for the past 50 years by those in a position to do anything about it.

Goldwater pointed out that federal funding would inevitably lead to federal control and that such control would result in ideological conformity. Goldwater advocated local control of education and an approach that focused on the training of individual minds, rather than the "one-size-fits-all" mentality that seeks to educate students to a certain mean level.

Most of us can detail how our lives were changed for the better by a teacher we can still remember, decades later. Unfortunately, education in our country today has turned away from the teacher and toward federal regulations that direct virtually everything that happens in classrooms across America. We have to return control of the schools to local communities and, ultimately, to parents. Good teachers should not fear such involvement; in my experience, the vast majority of teachers would welcome it.

Fifty years ago, Goldwater saw the virtue of this approach. His chapter on education ends on a prophetic note:

> [I]f we would improve education in America—and advance the fortunes of freedom—we will not rush to the Federal treasury with requests for money. We will focus attention on our local community, and make sure that our schools, private and public, are performing the job the Nation has the right to expect of them.

Of course, under Lyndon B. Johnson and his successors, our

country went in the other direction, politicizing public education and dumbing down the curriculum.

The George W. Bush administration, with its gimmicky "No Child Left Behind" (NCLB) federal educational mandates, has increased federal control over education dramatically and made it a lot harder to undo. That the Bush administration did not understand that their "proposed fix" would only make the situation worse is reflected in the remarks of Education Secretary Margaret Spellings as NCLB came up for renewal by Congress in 2006: "I talk about No Child Left Behind like Ivory Soap: It's 99.9 percent pure of something. There's not much needed in the way of change."

Yet a majority of states complained that what they got from NCLB was simply more unfunded federal mandates. Utah stood up to this latest federal attack on local control over education by passing a law "defying the Bush administration's No Child Left Behind Act despite a warning from the federal education secretary . . . that it could cost $76 million in federal aid," the Associated Press reported on May 2, 2005.

The Utah law, supported by Gov. Jon Huntsman and the overwhelming majority of Utah legislators, gave "Utah's education standards priority over federal requirements of the No Child Left Behind Act. It lets education officials ignore provisions of federal law that conflict with the state's program."

Utah's action was an encouraging sign that not all hope is lost. There remains some resistance at the grassroots level to the idea that so-called experts like Secretary Spellings know what's best for all of us when it comes to educating our children.

Federal power and funds for education need to be returned to the states and local communities with no strings attached. That is federalism—the core genius of the American constitutional system.

In the case of public education in America, there is no more fundamental principle than "We the People." Conservatives can best bring reform to our public-school systems by returning control over schools, including curricula and administration, to local communities. Too much emphasis has been put lately on making sure that students "feel good about themselves." What we need instead is a sense of accomplishment and pride in performance, and that can only come through the encouragement of a competitive spirit, among both students and teachers. Good students should be recognized and rewarded for superior performance, and so should good teachers.

Such a change would require not only a different vision of what education is about but a fairly fundamental shift in resources. Conservatives should champion a future in which the federal government in general, and the federal Department of Education in particular, have a much smaller role in public education. Parents in local communities should be empowered with genuine oversight over the administration of the schools in which their children study. Habits acquired by federal "experts" over the past 40 years or so will be hard to break. They have come to think of themselves as better informed and better able to make decisions about what is good for American students.

Many parents today attended schools that had already been removed from local control. So returning the primary responsibility for their children's education to them will be a new experience. But that experience will be beneficial to families and to the communities in which they live. Some special interests might rush to the microphones in protest, but conservatives who embrace "family values" must defend American families.

Our current educational system tries to be all things to all children. This has led to a teaching to the mean, a "dumbing down" of the quality of public education, beginning in the grade schools. In my home state of Texas, a study of high-school graduates taking the ACT in 2004 found that only 18 percent had the necessary skills for college and work. Many college freshmen are in need of remedial education. According to a survey conducted by Hart Research Associates and Public Opinion Strategies, college instructors report that 42 percent of entering freshmen are unprepared for college work, and employers estimate that 45 percent of recent high-school graduates entering the workforce lack necessary skills.

High-school graduates need to have the foundational skills for college and work. That requires a solid emphasis on core subject matter in secondary schools. Both workers going into the trades and students planning on attending a four-year college need a solid foundation in reading, writing, math, and science. Otherwise, they are going to remain unskilled workers with lower pay and fewer opportunities.

Those who go on to four-year colleges often gravitate to the "soft" majors, which have proliferated in recent decades. Tom Luce, a former assistant secretary at the U.S. Department of Education, points out that "America now graduates more sports exercise majors than electrical engineers," adding that "there were twice as many physics graduates in 1965 as in 2004."

Yet, as Mary Ann Rankin and William Brinkley wrote in a commentary for the *Austin American Statesman* (December 22, 2008), "American demand for scientists and engineers is expected to grow four times faster than all other professions over the next decade, according to the US Bureau of Labor Statistics. Yet today only 5 percent of US College undergraduates earn degrees in science and engineering, whereas in China, 42 percent of students do."

There is a huge mismatch between the areas of study that students are pursuing in college and the jobs that are available for college graduates. There is a similar mismatch with respect to the skilled trades. Too many high-school graduates are being told that they have to go to a four-year college in order to get ahead. In many cases, they would be better served by getting skills training at two-year technical institutes or through advanced-certification programs. Community colleges or qualified job-training organizations could develop programs that provide graduates with certification that they have received the training necessary to enter a particular field.

For example, you want to make sure that a newly hired construction worker has the ability to do the job. One way is for the worker to present a certificate showing that he trained according to a curriculum designed by an organization like the National Center for Construction Education and Research (NCCER) of Gainesville, Florida. NCCER is a 12-year-old nonprofit organization created by leaders in the construction industry to help ensure that tomorrow's workers receive the specialized training and preparation they need.

NCCER created a curriculum to fit standards developed by the construction industry as a whole. It is a national curriculum, consistent with federal guidelines. Graduates acquire portable skills. What qualifies them for work in the state of Texas qualifies them also in many other states.

A document certifying skills training of a higher order is a point of pride for the one who carries it. It tells the world he or she knows the job and how to do it—the very same message a college diploma is meant to convey.

According to NCCER, U.S. schools are not "preparing young people for the career opportunities that are available in our workplace." Their study points out that "28% of today's ninth graders will complete college, but only 20% of the jobs will require a four-year degree . . . 32% of the population will have the necessary skills that 65% of the jobs will require." Ed Prevatt, senior manager for workforce development at NCCER, told me that 275,000 construction jobs go unfilled every year because of a lack of worker training. And that is before the baby boomers, some 75 million strong, begin retiring in large numbers. (Prevatt also touts a study which shows that high-school graduates with NCCER training earn, over a lifetime, $375,000 more than they would without it.)

What works in construction would work with all skilled trades. And nearly all trades today are skilled. Technology sets the pace. Gone are the days when a strong back was the only qualification one needed for many American jobs. Nuclear development, nursing, refinery operation, computer science, the whole roster of modern jobs—they require a knowledge of the basics combined with appropriate skills training.

Job preparation can be tied to an existing secondary school, community college, apprenticeship program, or qualified job-training provider. The time necessary to complete it can be a matter of months or two years or more, depending on the difficulty or technical nature of the particular job.

Having a recognizable skill and using one's talents to fill demands in the workforce is my definition of a "good job." Work boosts the worker's morale, giving him a sense of purpose in life and a reason to get out of bed in the morning. Proficiency in a skilled trade can be a path to a secure economic future, even in difficult times like these.

It is high time we got over the notion that a four-year college degree is the only piece of paper that indicates a person's potential for success. No well-trained worker is a second-class citizen. He or she can contribute to the economic well-being of our society.

The skills required for so-called blue-collar jobs (I call them "open collar" jobs) are impressive, and they allow young workers to make a good living and raise a family. Even in an economic downturn, the demand for skilled workers remains strong because there is such a shortage.

Compare these opportunities for good-paying jobs with this disturbing statistic cited by career counselor Marty Nemko: "Among high school students who graduated in the bottom 40 percent of their classes and whose first institutions were four-year colleges, two-thirds had not earned diplomas eight and a half years later." Are we setting young people up for failure by promoting the idea that a college education is the only ticket to the good life?

We cannot have a thriving economy in the long run without a well-educated citizenry and a skilled workforce. That skilled workforce requires a strong core of qualified engineers and scientists along with capable tradesmen and craftsmen. America is falling short on both fronts under our current educational system.

Moreover, we cannot have a skilled workforce without a strong work ethic. As chairman of the Texas Workforce Commission, I talk with employers around the state. They tell me how difficult it is to find and retain good workers. We seem to be losing that strong work ethic which was a distinctive feature of the American character. It is tempting to find fault with the current generation for this declining work ethic, but my own 60's generation bears a large share of the blame.

The 60's counterculture, with its emphasis on rights instead of responsibilities ("If it feels good, do it") and a sense of entitlement rather than the acceptance of obligations, has done much to undermine the importance of hard work as the key to success in life.

Charles Murray, the author of *Real Education*, argues that there are "Four Simple Truths for Bringing America Back to Reality": ability varies; half of the children are below average; too many people are going to college; we have to do a better job of educating the academically gifted.

All of us have different talents. The question is how to use properly the talents God has given us. Even if someone has a high IQ and enormous intellectual potential, that ability can be neglected or

174

used improperly. Those individuals who use their talents to become skilled tradesmen or craftsmen have much to be proud of and should not be considered second-class citizens. As Murray writes:

> Finding a good carpenter, painter, electrician, plumber, glazier, mason—the list goes on and on—is difficult, and it is a seller's market. Journeymen craftsmen routinely make incomes in the top half of the income distribution while master craftsmen can make six figures. They have work even in a soft economy. Their jobs cannot be outsourced to India. And the craftsman's job provides wonderful intrinsic rewards that come from mastery of a challenging skill that produces tangible results. How many white-collar jobs provide nearly as much satisfaction?

The real problem, as Murray observes, is the education of the "elites" (politicians, businessmen, and intellectuals) who essentially run our country. They are not being taught the basic tenets of our Western Christian civilization, or even "the world's two most influential secular ethical systems, Aristotelian and Confucian":

> If your children grow up to be courageous, temperate, able to think clearly about the consequences of their actions, to be concerned with the welfare of others, with a sense of obligation to set a good example for others in their own behavior and to accord to others their rightful due—all of which are central tenets of both ethical systems—do you really care whether they were raised to be good Aristotelians or good Confucians?
>
> The problem is when they are raised in no tradition at all, and instead imbibe the reigning ethical doctrine of contemporary academia, nonjudgmentalism. If they were taught merely to be tolerant, fine. But nonjudgmentalism goes much further, proclaiming that it is a sin to make judgments about the relative merit of different ways of living. Nonjudgmentalism is the inverse of rigor in thinking about virtue—a task that, above all else, requires the formation of considered judgments.

We have a special obligation to teach those who will be leaders of our nation the importance of wisdom and the difference between right and wrong. Again, Murray says it much better than I could:

> We live in an age when it is unfashionable to talk about the special responsibility of being gifted, because to do so acknowledges inequality of ability, which is elitist, and inequality of responsibilities, which is also elitist. And so children who know they are smarter than the other kids tend, in a most human reaction, to think of themselves as superior to them. Because giftedness is not to be talked about, no one tells high-IQ children explicitly, forcefully and repeatedly that their intellectual talent is a gift. That they are not superior human beings, but lucky ones. That the gift brings with it obligations to be worthy of it. That among those obligations, the most important and most difficult is to aim not just at academic accomplishment, but at wisdom.
>
> The encouragement of wisdom requires a special kind of education. It requires first of all recognition of one's own intellectual limits and fallibilities—in a word, humility. This is perhaps the most conspicuously missing part of today's education of the gifted. Many high-IQ students, especially those who avoid serious science and math, go from kindergarten through an advanced degree without ever having a teacher who is dissatisfied with their best work and without ever taking a course that forces them to say to themselves, "I can't do this." Humility requires that the gifted learn what it feels like to hit an intellectual wall, just as all of their less talented peers do, and that can come only from a curriculum and pedagogy designed especially for them. That level of demand cannot fairly be imposed on a classroom that includes children who do not have the ability to respond. The gifted need to have some classes with each other not to be coddled, but because that is the only setting in which their feet can be held to the fire.
>
> The encouragement of wisdom requires mastery of analytical building blocks. The gifted must assimilate the details of grammar and syntax and the details of logical fallacies not because they will need them to communicate in

daily life, but because these are indispensable for precise thinking at an advanced level.

The encouragement of wisdom requires being steeped in the study of ethics, starting with Aristotle and Confucius. It is not enough that gifted children learn to be nice. They must know what it means to be good.

We need to return to a classical liberal education.

The problem is that we have tenured too many radicals of my generation, men and women who are dead set against teaching the verities of Western civilization. Jesse Jackson's refrain—"Hey hey, ho ho, Western culture's got to go"—sums up the mind-set of the deconstructionists who control the liberal-arts curriculum of our most prestigious colleges and universities. And when a scholar like Dr. Robert Koons attempts to establish a program teaching the classics at the undergraduate level at an institution like the University of Texas at Austin, he is met with strong resistance by leftist professors determined to deprive students of the opportunity to learn from the classical authors of Western civilization. All too often, students with an intellectual curiosity are not even being exposed to professors who have a sense of, much less an appreciation of, the achievements of Western civilization.

My friend Tiemann ("Skipper") Dippel, Jr., has devoted much of his adult life to the study of what he calls "the language of conscience." Like Charles Murray, Skipper seeks to blend the Western ideas of the Golden Rule and the common good based on the natural law with Confucius's emphasis on instilling in leaders a sense of humility and the "morality of obligation and public service." As Dippel writes, Confucius sought to train "gentlemen" who would adhere to the "Silver Rule of obligation." Dippel calls these paths to true leadership (the Golden Rule of Christ and the Silver Rule of Confucius) "enlightened conservatism." Sadly, Tiemann Dippel has had more success in getting an audience for his ideas in communist China than at the University of Texas.

Much must change if we are to return to the guiding principles that once made America great.

A Return to

Constitutional Principles

"Where you have a concentration of power in a few hands,
all too frequently men with the mentality of gangsters get control."
~Lord Acton

How did it come to this? A republic that had in its earliest days such outstanding leaders as George Washington, John Adams, James Madison, Thomas Jefferson, and Alexander Hamilton has deteriorated into a crew of Washington politicians whose main concern is telling people what they want to hear in order to keep getting elected. Add to the mix totally ruthless men such as President Obama's White House Chief of Staff Rahm Emanuel, and it makes me wonder if our republic will be able to survive our latest set of crises. Of course, our country is at such great risk because we abandoned our constitutional principles sometime ago.

I have known a number of statesmen who have risen above narrow partisanship and concern about winning the next election to do the right thing for our country, but there seem to be fewer in Washington these days. We won the Cold War because we could still rely on such outstanding presidents as Dwight David Eisenhower and Ronald Reagan at critical moments in that conflict. When I worked on Capitol Hill during my student days at Georgetown University, there were still many senators and congressmen, Democrats and Republicans alike, who were willing to base their legislative decisions on what was good for the country. Lobbyists had not yet assumed dominance on the Washington political scene. These days, however, running for Congress or for the presidency is all about raising big money to win office and making deals with powerful special interests to get elected—and then to stay in office.

No wonder politics, particularly at the national level, seems to attract more and more people interested in gaining and keeping power, rather than men and women who are dedicated to advancing the good of their communities, their states, and our country. When the Republicans controlled Congress in recent years, Americans already had a low regard for the institution. Approval ratings are even lower now that the Democrats are in charge. The American people seem to be saying, "A pox on both your houses."

In times past, the people would have thrown such weak characters out of office. The Founding Fathers knew that the people were best served when their representatives lived among them and were subject to frequent elections. In the last half of the 20th century, however, air conditioning came to Washington, and that allowed Congress to be in session virtually year-round.

The longer congressmen are in Washington, the more they spend. The 51st Congress, which sat from March 1889 to March 1891, was excoriated for years because it was the first Congress to spend one billion dollars during its term. Now the Congress spends about two billion dollars each day, and no one bats an eye.

Politicians today move to Washington as soon as they win their first election. Suddenly, they are no longer going to church with their spouses and children in their home districts. While the congressmen are home campaigning, their families are going to church in suburban Washington. They send their children to expensive private schools. The children's classmates are not from their parents' home districts; they are the sons and daughters of other politicians, foreign diplomats, and wealthy lobbyists. When the representative goes home, he does not sit in the stands and watch his children play with his home team. He is on stage, all weekend, while his children are playing with their neighbors in Maryland or Virginia. Talk about losing touch! In order to make sure that the voters do not throw them out, politicians of both parties team up to gerrymander their districts so that, in any given election, only ten percent of the 435 congressional seats are even in play.

It is time we had term limits for members of Congress, with a maximum of 12 years of service in either the U.S. House or the Senate.

Matters that traditionally were within the purview of our legislative bodies, such as the recognition of God in the public square, the right to life of the unborn, and the structure of our electoral systems at the state and local level, have been taken over by unelected federal judges with lifetime tenure under the guise of interpreting the Constitution.

We have gone far afield from the constitutional system described in the *Federalist*, with its separation of powers combined with checks and balances at the federal level. As conceived by the Founding Fathers, Congress has the final say in any dispute among the three branches of government. Its powers were broadly defined in Article I of the Constitution. The Framers of the Constitution had a healthy fear of tyranny, so they restricted the power of the president, and they never intended to place much power in the hands of judges who were appointed for life.

That sensible political structure also included strict limits on the national government. The Founding Fathers emphasized the principle of federalism—wherever possible, power should be reserved to the states, and to the people themselves. The notion of "express powers" meant that the federal government was restricted to those powers delegated to it by the states.

Recent generations of schoolchildren have not learned these principles of federalism. How could they? After all, our public-school system is heavily influenced these days by the National Education Association (NEA), one of the most powerful lobbying organizations in America. Its goals include increasing the centralization of power over education in Washington, D.C. The NEA views local control over education as an outdated relic of an archaic constitutional system. The *Federalist* was originally published in newspapers as a series of op-ed pieces designed to sway the debate in New York over the ratification of the Constitution. Most of the people reading them had little trouble understanding the frequent references to classical writers and works. I wonder how many teachers could make sense of them today?

As public interest in the Constitution, the separation of powers, and the very concept of federalism diminishes, our elected officials no longer feel compelled either to address them or to act according to their principles. Our public debates, even over such momentous decisions as whether to go to war, no longer make reference to those principles.

No matter which party is in charge, members of Congress simply argue over how much the federal government will grow—and how quickly. Congress participates in its own destruction by transferring more and more of its powers to the executive and judicial branches. The Framers intended Congress to be the preeminent branch of the federal government. That is no longer the case, in spite of Congress's lavish spending habits.

Speaking of federal spending, unless we get a responsible fiscal policy in place at the national level, any hope of returning to our constitutional form of government is simply wishful thinking. Too many of our elected and appointed officials think that they are spending "other people's money," when they should be treating spending requests as they would in their own businesses and households.

The idea that the federal government is going to spend its way out of our current economic difficulties reminds me of what Charles Prince, the former CEO of Citigroup, said in an interview with the *Financial Times* in July 2007, shortly before the credit excesses caught up with our major Wall Street institutions: "When the music stops, . . . things will be complicated. But as long as the music is playing, you've got to get up and dance. We're still dancing." Four months later, Prince was out of a job; over the next year, the U.S. taxpayers bailed out Citigroup to the tune of $326 billion, as we paid for the mistakes of Chuck Prince, Robert Rubin, and other key executives of that institution.

For government as well as for the financial industry, the music has stopped, and we are paying a heavy price for the spending excesses of our federal government. We cannot run $700 to $800 billion trade deficits annually, and trillion dollar and larger budget deficits, while bailing out troubled financial institutions to the tune of trillions of additional dollars, without serious consequences. The budget deficit in the first year of the Obama administration is expected to be in the range of two trillion dollars. How long can we expect foreign nations to continue to buy our debt, even as our currency declines in value?

We have to act before it is too late. The federal government should be required to balance its budget annually except in times of recession or war. As former Reagan official John Cogan notes, "[D]uring the first ninety years of U.S. history, spending authority was concentrated in a single committee in each house of Congress, and budgets were balanced except during recessions and wars." In fact, for most of our history before 1940, the federal budget was balanced every year.

Cogan has the right remedy. Congress needs to reassert its "authority to report all appropriations" through a single appropriations committee or a budget committee. Under our current system, with dozens of various committees having the ability to authorize spending as they see fit, there is no spending accountability. Cogan cites Congressman Samuel Randell, chairman of the House Appropriations Committee in 1884: "If you undertake to divide all these appropriations and have many committees where there ought to be but one, you will enter upon a path of extravagance you cannot foresee the length of or the depth of until we find the Treasury of the country bankrupt."

While liberals always seem to want to increase the size of government and to spend more of our tax dollars, conservatives once made fiscal responsibility and balanced budgets the cornerstone of our economic philosophy. That changed in the late 1970's with the adoption of "supply-side economics," which downplayed the importance of controlling spending when cutting taxes. Supply-siders such Jack Kemp and Art Laffer claimed that we could grow our way out of deficits with tax cuts alone. While lower tax rates do spur economic growth, that is not sufficient to balance the budget. We need to consider the spending side of the equation as well. As late as 2002, Vice President Dick Cheney told Treasury Secretary Paul O'Neill that "deficits don't matter" when O'Neill tried to warn Cheney of the looming fiscal crisis.

While I was a strong proponent of President Reagan's across-the-board tax cuts in 1981, I also believed that we had to control spending to keep the budget in balance. We did that in the agency I headed, Action, where our motto was "Doing more with less." However, the spending cuts made there and at some other agencies and departments during Reagan's first term were the exception rather than the rule.

The supply-siders never appreciated the connection between limiting spending and lowering taxes. Yet the two greatest political leaders of the modern conservative movement, Barry Goldwater and Ronald Reagan, understood that connection well.

Returning to a balanced federal budget would impose a badly needed fiscal discipline on Congress and the executive branch. Rather than basing spending on our "wish list," the federal government would be forced to spend only what it takes in through taxes. That would force us to establish priorities.

One means of bringing federal spending under control would be for Congress to return both the responsibility and the money it collects for most domestic programs to the states and local communities. Bloc-granting Medicaid back to the states would be a good place to start. If present trends continue, Medicaid spending may bankrupt many state governments. Letting each state determine how it wants to implement healthcare programs for the poor makes sense economically and socially. One size does not fit all.

Other domestic spending areas, such as education, housing, transportation, job training, and social services, should be returned to the purview of the states and local communities. Money would be returned to the states and communities so that they could establish their own spending priorities. Earmarks and the game of trying to get funding for one's favored projects would be a thing of the past. Cities, school districts, universities, and states no longer would have to send their representatives and lobbyists to Washington, D.C., hat in hand, to get their piece of the federal pie.

I went back into government in 2007 for the first time since my days in the Reagan administration. Gov. Rick Perry asked me to serve as the chairman of the Texas Workforce Commission (TWC), the state equivalent of the federal Department of Labor. I was amazed at how much of the budget of our agency consists of mandated expenditures by the federal government and how little discretion we have regarding a variety of programs that fall under the purview of the TWC. "With federal aid comes federal control" is even more true today than it was back when I was the director of Action in the early 1980's—and it was a serious problem at that time.

Returning control and funding of such programs to states and local communities would free congressmen from having to spend so much of their time "bringing home the bacon" for their constituents and special interests. Congress could actually concentrate on such fundamental issues as border security, balancing the budget, tax policy, Social Security reform, energy and healthcare policy, judicial reform, immigration reform, and defense spending.

Shifting funding and control of much of our domestic spending back to the states and localities would have other beneficial effects. The influence of the K Street lobby would be greatly diminished. And congressmen would feel less pressure from their major contributors and other special interests.

Congress could reassume its constitutional role as the most important branch (and the ultimate decisionmaker when there is a conflict among the three branches) of the federal government.

Congress could also help restore our constitutional principles by putting an end to judicial supremacy. Much of the damage done in the last 50 years has been inflicted by the federal courts, that part of our constitutional system that the Framers referred to as "the least dangerous branch." In recent decades, "The Supremes" have become the primary source of new legislation—disguised, of course, as legal opinions addressing specific cases.

Conservative scholarship on the courts over the past 40 years has decried the "tyranny of the judiciary." Congress's traditional role of deciding political questions has been arrogated by unelected federal judges who have substituted their will for the will of the people. Both houses of Congress have gone along with this deviation from the Constitution, with disastrous results. Politicians find that it is all too easy to let the Supreme Court and lower federal courts handle such tough questions as abortion, school prayer, and racial discrimination. The representative can simply tell the folks back home that "it's the court's fault, not mine."

The federal courts have issued an avalanche of revolutionary opinions on issues ranging from school prayer to abortion to religious rights. These justices have appointed themselves as the arbiters of political decisions that the Framers deemed to be the province of the Congress.

Since the *Roe* v. *Wade* decision in 1973, conservative elected officials and grassroots activists have spent millions of dollars and thousands of hours advocating constitutional amendments that would guarantee the right to life. Unfortunately liberals, led by the ACLU, have succeeded in making support for abortion and homosexual rights virtual requirements for membership in the Democratic Party. Given the current political lay of the land, any effort to buttress traditional family values through a constitutional amendment is doomed to failure.

Even today, a majority of the American people is solidly pro-life and believes that marriage is the union of one man and one woman. My own sense is that support for the left's extreme views regarding homosexual unions and abortion will wane in coming years, and that the grandchildren of today's cultural leftists will agree with their great-great-grandparents—the parents of two generations ago who instinctively supported the protection of life at all stages and traditional marriage and the natural family as the basic institutions of a civilized society.

In the short run, though, conservatives must fight to protect human life and traditional family values. We should have no qualms about invoking the constitutional powers of Congress to address radical judicial decisions. The Framers gave to Congress the power not only to establish the federal courts, but to define and to limit their jurisdiction.

Left-wing constitutional law professors have long been aware of the ticking time bomb of Article III, Section 2, which allows Congress to limit the questions that the federal courts can even entertain. For years these professors have told their law students that this provision, while constitutional, is actually revolutionary, dangerous, and should never be employed by rational men. Nonetheless, Congress routinely limits the jurisdiction of the federal courts in noncontroversial regulatory bills that might be tied up for years by challenges in federal court.

Supreme Court justices have long envied Congress's power to decide political issues. The Framers recognized the danger of placing the power to make political decisions in the branch that was most isolated from the will of the people. Wisely, they did not put it there. Unwisely, over the past 50 years, Congress has allowed the courts to assume that power so that our representatives do not have to take the heat for making difficult political decisions.

Still, we have a remedy in Article III, Section 2, of the U.S. Constitution. Congress can simply reassert its duty to legislate on political issues by including in the text of appropriate legislation a section that prohibits the federal courts from hearing challenges to that legislation.

The beauty of this remedy lies in its simplicity. Congress can implement it with a majority vote. Of course, the restoration of congressional responsibility will cause an outcry from those leftists who use the federal courts to implement social policy. But a reinvigorated people, enjoying the restoration of their rights, can stand that kind of heat.

With the revival of the powers of Congress, we will see a revival of communities across America. A similar empowerment of families, and a resurgence of the democratic spirit, is within our grasp if we return to the tried and true principles of conservatism. Such a revival need not be revolutionary—in fact, it would help heal the country from the damage wrought by the revolution in our political culture over the past 50 years. Conservatives understand that no legislature can restore the moral fiber and culture of the nation. However, we also understand that the Framers provided us with certain safeguards to defend our way of life against assaults by renegade federal courts.

But we cannot stop with the courts. We also need to address the dangers of the "imperial presidency."

When I was a college student during the Kennedy years, James McGregor Burns, a liberal professor, wrote a best-selling book entitled *The Deadlock of Democracy*. Burns argued that we needed a strong president to override the inherent conservatism of Congress, an institution that, in his view, was thwarting the will of the American people. These days, it is such neoconservatives and "national greatness" Republicans as Dick Cheney, Newt Gingrich, and former George W. Bush speechwriter Michael Gerson who are the leading proponents of a strong executive. After September 11, Vice President Cheney's office argued in favor of a "unitary executive." George Carey, a former professor of government at

Georgetown University, describes this constitutional theory:

> On the basis of Article II, section 1, the theory holds that the
> inherent powers embodied in the Commander-in-Chief clause
> belong exclusively to the president; that those powers cannot
> be modified, altered, or in any way diminished by Congress or
> the judiciary. Thus, the inherent or implied executive powers
> are shielded from the other branches with their nature and
> extent, following the logic of the unitary executive theory, being
> matters for the President alone to determine.

There is a certain irony in the fact that two political factions (neo-conservatives and welfare-state liberals) that supposedly are at odds with one another on a number of political issues are in agreement when it comes to their belief in the "necessity" of such an "expansive" view of presidential powers. These two factions simply have different ideas of what they want their strong president to do.

That should not surprise anyone who has studied the underlying political philosophies of these two factions. The roots of both are essentially liberal—Cheney, Paul Wolfowitz, and their neoconservative allies were never philosophical conservatives. Dick Cheney was first a Rumsfeld/Ford Republican, before becoming closely aligned with the neoconservatives as George W. Bush's vice president, and Paul Wolfowitz is neither an economic nor a social conservative.

The views of the neoconservatives on the proper role of government in our lives have more in common with those of presidents Franklin Delano Roosevelt (the architect of the New Deal) and Lyndon Baines Johnson (who gave us the Great Society) than with the beliefs of Barry Goldwater and Ronald Reagan. In fact, those two Democratic presidents were much admired by the neo-cons while Barry Goldwater was reviled by them back when he first emerged as the standard-bearer for the modern conservative movement. (Neoconservative Seymour Martin Lipset all but called Goldwater, who was half-Jewish, a neo-Nazi in the early 1960's.)

After he left the Bush White House, Michael Gerson wrote a book called *Heroic Conservatism*. It reveals the mind-set of those who favor "national greatness" conservatism, which is simply a rebranding of big-government conservatism. In reviewing Gerson's book for the *Wall Street Journal*, John Hulsman did not see much that could be called "conservative": Gerson, Hulsman writes, "calls for the Republican Party to redefine itself and brighten its future by casting aside its suspicion of big government and pursuing lofty projects of statist dogoodery. Let us hope that Republicans ignore him."

Contrast Gerson's enthusiasm for "national greatness" conservatism with Barry Goldwater's view of the Constitution and the appropriate role for the federal government. What would be left of conservatism if Gerson and his ilk succeeded in beating the liberals in expanding the size and power of the federal government? Nothing more than the smug self-satisfaction of having triumphed in an ideological battle in which true conservative principles were utterly destroyed.

The answer lies not in Gerson's aggrandizement of government, but in its opposite. Here is how Goldwater put it in *The Conscience of a Conservative* in 1960:

> The time will come when we entrust the conduct of our affairs to the men who understand that their first duty as public officials is to divest themselves of the power that they have been given. It will come when Americans, in hundreds of communities throughout the nation, decide to put the man in office who is pledged to enforce the Constitution and restore the Republic.

Goldwater wanted to reduce the power of the federal government, not expand it.

It is not just traditional conservatives like myself who are suspicious of the growing power of the imperial presidency. Libertarians and old-style liberals are also worried about the loss of civil liberties as presidential powers are expanded with little regard for the separation of powers.

Naomi Wolf, a liberal advisor to the presidential campaigns of Bill Clinton and Al Gore, warns of this loss of freedom in her most recent book, *End of America: Letter of Warning to a Young Patriot*. Her words are echoed by conservative scholar George Carey, who saw troubling signs in the push by former vice president Dick

Cheney for a more expansive view of presidential power, "not subject to abrogation or modification by legislative authority." For Carey, "this justification of presidential powers leads straightaway to an 'imperial presidency' and the breakdown of the constitutional separation of powers."

Although of very different philosophical persuasions, both Wolf and Carey believe that Congress is losing the battle to rein in the imperial presidency. Does anyone seriously believe that President Obama and White House Chief of Staff Rahm Emanuel will be any less likely than Bush and Cheney to expand executive power?

The problem is twofold: First, Congress has never seriously challenged the imperial presidency. Congressmen would rather spend their time catering to the special interests that fund their reelection campaigns and setting themselves up for a career as a Washington lobbyist after they leave Congress. Second, advocates of a strong executive do not seem to realize that the reassertion of the constitutional role of Congress would strengthen the legitimate powers of the executive at the very moment when those powers are under fire from all directions.

Consider the war in Iraq. If President Bush had gone to Congress in 2002 and got a declaration of war against Iraq, the vicissitudes of the invasion, war, and occupation would have been much less disconcerting to the American people. The legitimacy conferred by a constitutional declaration of war is not merely symbolic.

By shunning its constitutional role in the debate over whether to go to war in Iraq, Congress solidified the idea in the public's mind that Congress is largely irrelevant when it comes to matters of war and peace. Those decisions, everyone seems to believe, are for the president to make. Yet the circumventing of Congress's authority to declare war weakens the presidency itself. When things go badly (as they have in Iraq), Congress has no stake in defending the original decision to go to war.

The antidote to the imperial presidency lies in the U.S. Constitution, and specifically in the role of Congress. Politicians often talk about defending our constitutional rights, but few seem to have read Article I, which specifies the legislative powers of Congress, and Article II, which sets forth the powers of the president. Reading the Constitution and the *Federalist* makes it clear how concerned the Framers were about power becoming concentrated in the hands of the executive.

George Carey notes that James Madison, one of the authors of the *Federalist*, believed that "the very existence of a concentration of powers constitutes tyranny." As Madison wrote, "The accumulation of all powers, legislative, executive and judicial, in the same hands whether of one, a few, or many and whether hereditary, self-appointed or elective, may justly be pronounced the very definition of tyranny."

Article I, Section 8, of the U.S. Constitution sets out in great detail the broad powers of the Congress. While Congress has the final say in any dispute it might have with the executive and judicial branches of the federal government, it has allowed both of those branches to assume powers that were originally vested in Congress. Congress simply needs to take those powers back. George Carey notes that "Congress has the authority to police and control the other branches. It can, for example, impeach and remove the president and judges, override presidential vetoes, control the appellate jurisdiction of the Supreme Court."

By contrast, the executive power, spelled out in Article II, Section 2, of the Constitution, was "carefully limited, both in extent and duration," as James Madison states in *Federalist* 48. The Founding Fathers did not want to get rid of arbitrary rule by the king of England only to succumb to similar rule by a king in the United States.

The defenders of the theory that the powers of the presidency are virtually unlimited, especially in wartime, assert that the executive powers conferred on the president are not limited at all by the specificity of Article II. Instead, they argue, those executive powers refer to powers developed over the centuries that were well known to the delegates to the Constitutional Convention in 1787 and to the state conventions that ratified the Constitution.

These arguments are, to put it plainly, simply false. Long before the Magna Carta, the powers of the English king were limited, as the crown itself acknowledged. Only with the development of the "divine right of kings," hundreds of years after Magna Carta, did tyrannical monarchs claim total power. Louis XIV of France insisted that he was the state (*l'etat, c'est moi*) and thus did not need to consult any other power, human or divine.

This claim to total power was affirmed in theory by Thomas Hobbes' *Leviathan* in the 17th century—a tumultuous period filled with constant war, revolution, and terror—and in the 18th century by Jean-Jacques Rousseau's *Social Contract*, whose totalitarian message spawned the French Revolution and Robespierre's Reign of Terror. Indeed, Claes Ryn, a political theorist at the Catholic University of America, has branded the neocons "the new Jacobins," a reference to the most fervent French Revolutionaries who sent thousands to the guillotines for what George Orwell would call "thoughtcrime."

The American Revolution was fought to restore to the colonists the rights of freeborn Englishmen. The Framers of the Constitution had no intention of establishing a new tyrant on this side of the Atlantic. The Tenth Amendment to the Constitution—the "forgotten amendment" that conservatives would do well to remember—makes it clear: "The powers not delegated to the United States by the Constitution, nor prohibited by it to the States, are reserved to the States respectively, or to the people." So much for the myth of unlimited executive power.

The Framers conferred specific powers on the president: He is "Commander in Chief of the Army and Navy of the United States." Yet he does not have the power to declare war; only Congress does. The president can enter into treaties with foreign countries, but those treaties must be approved by a two-thirds vote of the U.S. Senate. He can appoint ambassadors, federal judges, and the heads of agencies, commissions, and departments of the federal government. But even those nominations have to be approved by a majority vote of the U.S. Senate.

That is the extent of the president's power under the Constitution. While he can recommend to Congress "such measures as he shall judge necessary and expedient," Congress does not even need to consider such proposals, much less rubber stamp them. For all else, the president must rely on a specific grant of power from Congress or on those powers that are implied by such a grant.

Some may take umbrage at such a narrow construction of the constitutional powers of the president in these perilous times.

Islamic radicalism poses at least as serious a threat to our way of life as that posed by communism during Barry Goldwater's day. Moreover, while the Soviet Union infiltrated our government with spies and fellow travelers such as Alger Hiss, the Soviets never launched suicide bombings against prominent targets in the United States. Aren't the words of Barry Goldwater that I previously cited—"The time will come when we entrust the conduct of our affairs to the men who understand that their first duty as public officials is to divest themselves of the power that they have been given"—outdated and irrelevant in light of the dangers we face?

In effect, what the supporters of the unitary executive wish to do is to destroy our Constitution in order to save our way of life. But if we heed their advice and throw out the Constitution, then what will be left to save of our way of life?

The best way to preserve our country is to return to the constitutional principles of separation of powers and checks and balances. The war-powers clause provides a case in point. It is Congress, not the president, which has the constitutional authority to declare war and to raise and maintain our military forces. No President should seek to circumvent the will of Congress and the language of the Constitution by sending our young men and women off to fight in foreign lands without the specific authorization of Congress. If the war is truly in our national interest, then Congress—and the American people—will support the president's recommendation.

In a similar vein, it is Congress, not the president, that has the authority to enter into treaties that regulate commerce with foreign countries. Yet the two Bush administrations and the Clinton administration have negotiated a broad range of so-called free-trade agreements with very little input from Congress. If such treaties are in the best interest of our nation, then Congress needs to be engaged in the process from the very beginning, and the American people need to be informed of the impact such treaties may have on their jobs and on our economy in general before these agreements become "done deals."

We have to put partisanship and short-term political advantage aside in this dispute over executive *versus* legislative power. The stakes are too high. Both Democrats and Republicans have become almost slavish in their support for the expansion of executive powers whenever their respective party holds the White House.

Republicans in Congress acted much more independently (and more like the conservatives they were supposed to be) when Bill Clinton was in the White House than when George H.W. Bush or George W. Bush was president.

Congressional Republicans, who opposed Clinton's bombing of Serbia because it was not in our national interest, almost uniformly supported George W. Bush's decision to launch a pre-emptive war in Iraq. Many congressional Democrats, who backed Clinton's military actions, have turned against the "Republican" War in Iraq. Would they have acted the same had Clinton decided to take out Saddam Hussein?

Congressional Republicans were diligent about controlling federal spending during the Clinton presidency, but they spent with abandon during George W. Bush's eight years in office. We conservatives have to stand for constitutional principles and against the imperial presidency no matter which party controls the White House. We need to encourage Congress to reassert its constitutional role as the preeminent branch of the federal government. One way to accomplish this is for the U.S. Senate to reassert its own executive powers. Few Americans are aware that the Senate meets regularly in executive session to consider nominations to executive and diplomatic posts, and to give its advice and consent to treaties. The Senate needs to reassert its proper role as a check and balance on the executive branch.

Returning power from Washington, D.C., to the states and local communities is essential if we are to save our country from sliding into socialism or a form of state capitalism in which our lives will be controlled from the cradle to the grave.

Traditional Values for a

New American Century

When I worked in the Reagan administration, I helped implement First Lady Nancy Reagan's "Just Say No To Drugs" campaign. It was a successful initiative to attack the demand side of the drug-abuse problem by discouraging young people from getting involved in the drug culture in the first place. It conveyed a clear message to young people that the use of illegal drugs was something to be avoided for many good reasons. The program worked because it helped young Americans realize the dangers of becoming trapped in the drug culture. We did this through sensible education that relied on good science and current medical information. The Reagans knew a thing or two about glamour from their Hollywood days, and they knew that the glamour of the drug culture, often made appealing by the very films produced in Hollywood, was a strong force in recruiting new drug users.

Dr. Herbert Kleber told PBS's *Frontline*, "To diminish drug use, you need to de-glamorize and de-normalize drug use" in the manner of the "Just Say No" campaign, which "had a good effect in terms of decreasing from 33 percent to 12 percent, an enormous decrease." Indeed, according to Dr. Kleber, "1985-1986 turns out to be the high point of the cocaine epidemic." Unfortunately, Dr. Kleber noted that marijuana use increased rapidly again between 1992 and 1997. The rise in illegal drug use coincided with the end of the "Just Say No" program and the coming to power of the generation that was coming of age in the late 1960's, when drug use became fashionable in our youth culture.

I first became aware of the extent of the problem as an attorney in the 1970's in Dallas, Texas, representing young people facing criminal charges for illegal drug use. I saw too many lives wasted because impressionable young men thought that "doing drugs" was a cool thing.

197

Mrs. Reagan caught a lot of flack for the "Just Say No" campaign from the elites, who themselves were products of the pro-drug culture of the late 1960's. An article in *The Washington Monthly* called it the "Just Say Nonsense" program and accused Mrs. Reagan of "oversimplifying" a "complex problem." The magazine editorialized that we should encourage "responsible use" of illegal drugs. Tell that to those young Americans who succumbed to the allure of the drug culture and found it very difficult to extricate themselves once they were hooked.

Mrs. Reagan's campaign worked; illegal drug use fell dramatically during the Reagan presidency, and for a few years thereafter. That success shows the power of the bully pulpit and a strong, consistent message.

When I was a teenager in the late 1950's, everyone understood that getting involved with illegal drugs was a dumb thing to do. That attitude was part of our culture and accepted as a given, whether one was a Republican or a Democrat, a conservative or a liberal. All of that changed, however, with the countercultural assault on our traditional values in the late 1960's. And that assault was not just on the drug issue but across the board. And the counterculture of the 1960's has become the dominant culture of today.

It is time for a new generation of young Americans to recapture our culture on behalf of our traditional values.

The self-appointed leaders of today's culture—or what passes for culture these days—would have us believe that the cultivation of traditional virtues has no place in a modern, globalized world. These elites, safe in their penthouses in Hollywood, New York City, and Washington, D.C., tell us that honesty, fairness, hard work, modesty, honor, self-sacrifice, and good humor are outmoded relics of a previous age. Instead, the cultural elites rush to the defense of one of their own, filmmaker Roman Polanski, when authorities seek to extradite him to serve time for his criminal conviction for drugging, raping, and sodomizing a thirteen-year-old girl. To the elites, character does not count.

I disagree: The character we cultivate in our young people is as vital to the nation now as it was yesterday. If we do not recapture the founding ethic of America, then America will see her past glory and strength quickly erode.

All of our Founding Fathers—whatever their particular faith—knew that true liberty arises from a belief in God and a strong ethical compass. George Carey, my political-theory professor at Georgetown University, illustrates this foundation of the American political tradition by pointing to the first words of the Mayflower Compact, written by the Pilgrims before they even got off the boat: "In the Name of God, Amen." William Penn, the founder of Pennsylvania, was equally forceful in his faith: "Those who refuse to govern themselves by the laws of God will be ruled by tyrants."

Christian values are at the center of our national character, and the attack on them has taken a heavy toll on the traditional family. The intact family was the solid underpinning of our American culture for more than a dozen generations. My parents' generation faced hard economic times during the Great Depression. That generation held America together during that difficult period in no small part because of their deep sense of family, neighborhood, community, a strong work ethic, and an unwavering faith in God. Even today, as economist Thomas Sowell has discussed at length, the greatest asset in the effort of the poor to escape poverty is an intact family. Sadly, the vast majority of America's poor live in single-parent families.

The breakdown of the family stems from the abandonment of priorities that were once central to our culture. Today, if we declare something desirable on moral grounds, we will be assailed by certain secularists for being "too judgmental." This attitude goes by different names in different circles. Pope Benedict XVI has called it "the dictatorship of relativism." The intellectual heirs of the French Revolution would have us banish God and our religious beliefs from the public square.

Our country was not founded on relativism or the principles of the French Revolution but on the permanent truths that have served as the foundation of Western civilization for over two thousand years. If we are to find our way back to the sound principles that inform a free society, we must confront the curse of "diversity" head-on.

America has always had genuine diversity. It is reflected in our national motto, *e pluribus unum*. In the early days of our republic, there were, of course, atheists and others who did not embrace all the traditions and principles of the Founding Fathers. They were a minority, to be sure, but they also recognized that our country offered them bountiful opportunities precisely because it was founded on a belief in "the laws of nature and of nature's God." They were sufficiently educated in history and political theory to acknowledge that the ideological systems of atheists like Thomas Hobbes and Jean-Jacques Rousseau would destroy the very freedoms they enjoyed in America. We saw that in the rise of totalitarianism in the Soviet Union and elsewhere during the 20th century.

Unfortunately, our society has been under an increasingly lethal assault by a coalition of cultural ideologues who have not learned the lessons history offers about what has happened when men and societies have "forgotten God."

As our culture abandons basic truths and loses its moral compass, what will arise in its place? As Solzhenitsyn said, where falsehood reigns, violence will surely follow in its wake.

The Founding Fathers recognized that there would always be enemies of freedom. In fact, they understood that the greatest threat to freedom was not any foreign enemy, but the lust for power by which every politician is constantly tempted. In order to acquire that power, the ideologue will deform language. That is why Confucius said that the first step toward restoring order in a society that has lost its moorings is to restore the proper meaning of words. In the West, from Aristotle forward, the proper use of language has been recognized as a fundamental element of a society devoted to liberty.

Lenin said that one of his most important ideological tools was the dictionary, and Stalin wrote a famous piece on the use of vocabulary in ideology. Ho Chi Minh and Zhou Enlai both studied in Paris. They were not unenlightened peasants but intellectuals to the core. Like Karl Marx, who declared war on traditional philosophy in 1841, the modern left uses ideology and education as weapons in their efforts to destroy tradition and freedom. But the communist understanding of "education" is vastly different from our understanding. When the North Vietnamese communists took over in South Vietnam, one of the first things they did was to send their opponents and other dissenters to "re-education camps." What a contrast with the original purpose of a Harvard education: *Veritas*, Latin for "truth."

Our faith and our families are the indispensable foundations to a free society. It should be obvious to anyone who compares the America of the 1930's with the United States of today that these roots have been severely weakened. Our families then were prepared for the Great Depression—not with money, but with tenacity, devotion, dedication, and a profound faith and faithfulness. As our economic situation continues to deteriorate, the possibility of another Great Depression is not so far-fetched. How will we respond?

Unless we restore the moral foundations of our society, any attempt to fix our flawed economic system will be like applying a mere bandage to a gaping wound. Only a "virtuous people," the Founding Fathers believed, could preserve a free society. They had no illusions about human nature. "Men, they know, are great sinners, potentially prideful, lustful, deceiving even, though, also, happily, capable of a certain amount of virtue, which ought to be cultivated and developed," wrote Willmoore Kendall and George Carey in their discussion of the Constitution and the *Federalist* in their book *The Basic Symbols of the American Political Tradition.*

"Publius," as Kendall and Carey note, wrote that American people "shalt try, above all, to be a virtuous people, made up of virtuous individuals, because only a virtuous people can do justice, remain untyrannical, as it governs itself through deliberation about the general good."

While the economic, political, and cultural environment has worsened since President Reagan assumed office in 1981, the situation is not hopeless. I am convinced that the decline can be reversed with the right leadership and appropriate policies, but that is easier said than done. And we face challenges that earlier generations did not. Militant Islam is an even greater threat to Western civilization than that posed by the Soviet Union in the 20th century, and the United States remains uniquely positioned to provide the leadership necessary to prevail in that struggle.

Yet our culture has become saturated with self-indulgence, and politics has followed suit. Now we confront an enemy that is willing to die for its principles and which believes (perhaps rightly) that we are not.

America has to heed Socrates' admonition: "Know thyself." Right now, we are a house divided, and that simply cannot stand. We must decide whether we are going to step forward into this historic struggle as the vanguard of an increasingly materialist and declining West or as the last bastion of Christendom, confronting the enemy that has haunted it for centuries. Militant Muslims hate both decadent materialism and Christianity. But against militant Islam, Christianity will win; self-indulgent decadence will not.

Why must America lead this battle? Why not "the West"? The answer is as disconcerting as it is clear: Western Europe, decidedly post-Christian, is not up to the fight as it once was when it repelled the Islamic onslaught at the Battle of Lepanto. Nor is Russia likely to lead the way. Russia suffered throughout most of the 20th century under a communist system in which people had to live a lie every day just to survive. It will take a long time for the traditional religious roots of Russia and other Eastern European nations to grow again. And I fear that some of them may never grow back.

Will Asia lead the way as it emerges as an economic power? That is unlikely anytime soon. Asia seems infatuated with imitating the materialistic West; the Far East needs to discover that there is more to life than material riches if it is to become an effective ally in this battle.

That leaves the struggle against militant Islam up to the United States—and that means it is up to our generation of conservatives.

We are going to have to develop an effective strategy to address the rise of militant Islam. We are going to have to recruit allies, and that is going to take some work. But this is not an insurmountable task. There are many positive signs in this struggle. Yes, our religious faith has been weakened in recent decades, but it remains relatively strong. The majority of Americans instinctively recognize the threat to our way of life posed by militant Islam, and they know that it is not going away any time soon. In fact, it is not likely to go away until it is defeated.

The secular liberal answer to resurgent Islam is to encourage Muslims to emulate our materialistic, secular ways. Use our government's international broadcasting stations to bombard their children with rap music, and they will grow up to be just like us. This is not likely to sway the masses of Muslims for whom their faith is the center of their existence. In fact, it may drive more of their idealistic youth into the arms of militant, doctrinally pure radicals. The parents of suicide bombers are occasionally featured on Arab news broadcasts and websites, praising their dead children for their devotion to Islam.

The neoconservative answer to militant Islam is to use our military might to force the world to accept our ways. The neocons want to wage war throughout the Middle East to "make the world safe for democracy." Or, if that fails, we can kill them all.

The English historian Hilaire Belloc warned in the early 1930's that a resurgent Islam would threaten the West. Belloc was concerned that Western Europe, once the bastion of Christianity, was losing its faith while Islam was (in Belloc's words) "a very great religion physically paralyzed but morally intensely alive."

Belloc was writing at a time when fascism, Nazism, and communism were the dominant ideologies in Europe. He saw that all those materialist schemes were doomed to fail, yet Islam had an advantage: the timeless power of the spirit. "Will not perhaps the temporal power of Islam return and with it the menace of an armed Mohammedan world which will shake off the domination of Europeans—still nominally Christian—and reappear again as the prime enemy of our civilization?"

As Belloc well knew, not so long ago Islam came close to destroying Christianity by overrunning Europe: "It failed during the last years of the seventeenth century, only just over two hundred years ago. Vienna . . . was almost taken and only saved by the Christian army under the command of the King of Poland on a date that ought to be among the most famous in history— September 11, 1683."

Belloc's prediction has proved correct. So how should we respond to the challenge of a resurgent Islam?

We should heed Solzhenitsyn's call and combat the fervor of a resurgent Islam by returning to the neglected Christian roots of Western civilization and attempting to achieve greater Christian unity on matters of culture. Without a revitalized Christianity, militant Islam may well be the wave of the future.

There are Muslim enclaves outside of Paris today where French policemen do not dare show their faces. Muslims will dominate Western Europe before the end of this century if current demographic trends continue. And there is little sign that they will change: European birthrates are below replacement level, while Muslims in Europe continue to value large families.

In his landmark 1964 book *Suicide of the West*, James Burnham showed how secular liberalism had led to the weakening of Western civilization. In the intervening half-century, the situation has greatly deteriorated. The threat Burnham faced was communism, but his point applies just as well to our struggle with Islam. We must have a strong faith in our way of life, and a rootedness in the Christian Faith that once animated our civilization, if we are to survive and to defend ourselves against this foe.

Why does Pope Benedict XVI work so hard to reach out to other Christian believers? Because the Orthodox, traditional Anglicans, and evangelicals share his concern about the "dictatorship of relativism" in an increasingly secularized Europe. The re-Christianization of Europe and the reunification of Christians are necessary if the West is to rise to the challenge of resurgent Islam.

In his Regensburg Address, Pope Benedict called for rational discussion, not only with Islam, but with the secular powers of the West. True conservatism insists on a reasoned defense of the principles of ordered liberty—and insists that such liberty is itself reasonable.

Here at home, on every front—economic, political, and cultural—we are facing critical decisions that will set our course for generations to come. Some of these challenges are new; some have been growing for years. But if we are to avoid the fate of the Roman Empire, we have to face facts, ground our actions in reality, and set ourselves to work to rebuild our society.

If not us, who? If not now, when?

About the Author

A native Texan, Tom Pauken was elected national chairman of the College Republicans during the rise of the anti-Vietnam protest movement. Enlisting in the U.S. Army in 1967, Tom served as a military intelligence officer in Vietnam.

Tom served on President Ronald Reagan's White House staff. Named director of the Action agency by President Reagan, he eliminated the use of federal tax dollars to fund Saul Alinsky-style leftist organizers. At Action, Tom founded the Vietnam Veterans Leadership Program and implemented Nancy Reagan's "Just Say No to Drugs" campaign. For his meritorious service as director of Action, Tom Pauken was awarded the Ronald Reagan Medal of Honor by his fellow Reagan administration alumni.

Elected Texas Republican State Chairman in 1994, Tom helped build up a Republican majority in Texas from the grassroots.

A former venture-capital executive, Tom is a small business owner and the author of *The Thirty Years War: The Politics of the Sixties Generation*. He currently serves as chairman of the Texas Workforce Commission.